QUEBEC IN A GLOBAL LIGHT
Reaching for the Common Ground

Quebec in a Global Light

Reaching for the Common Ground

ROBERT CALDERISI

UNIVERSITY OF TORONTO PRESS
Toronto Buffalo London

ISBN 978-1-4875-0471-7

∞ Printed on acid-free paper with vegetable-based inks.

Munk Series on Global Affairs

Library and Archives Canada Cataloguing in Publication

Title: Quebec in a global light : reaching for the common ground / Robert
Calderisi.
Names: Calderisi, Robert, author.
Series: Munk series on global affairs.
Description: Series statement: Munk series on global affairs |
Includes bibliographical references and index.
Identifiers: Canadiana 2019005560X | ISBN 9781487504717 (hardcover)
Subjects: LCSH: Québec (Province) – Social conditions – 21st century. |
LCSH: Québec (Province) – Economic conditions – 21st century.
Classification: LCC FC2911 .C35 2019 | DDC 971.4/05—dc23

University of Toronto Press acknowledges the financial assistance to its
publishing program of the Canada Council for the Arts and the Ontario
Arts Council, an agency of the Government of Ontario.

Canada Council
for the Arts

Conseil des Arts
du Canada

ONTARIO ARTS COUNCIL
CONSEIL DES ARTS DE L'ONTARIO

an Ontario government agency
un organisme du gouvernement de l'Ontario

Funded by the
Government
of Canada

Financé par le
gouvernement
du Canada

Canadä

MIX
Paper from
responsible sources
FSC® C016245

For Geoffrey Adams (1926–2012),
who epitomized the best of the two cultures

Contents

Acknowledgments

Like many books, this one has a supporting cast. I am particularly grateful to the late Bernard Landry, the former Quebec premier (2001–2003), whose intellectual honesty, embrace of diversity, and clear-headed social democracy inspired me deeply. At his state funeral on 13 November 2018, one of his admirers, a man of Morrocan Jewish descent, said of him: "He loved Quebec too much not to want to share it with others." Pierre Fortin, one of Quebec's most prominent and pleasant economists, kept me focussed on the right issues and reassured me when I worried that my ambition was getting the better of me. Early on, a very patient Jean-François Payette introduced me to important aspects of *indépendantiste* thinking. As with my previous book, Jacques Gérin and Eric Southworth read every word of the manuscript. I also received good advice from Michel Arseneault, Richard Beaumier, my siblings (Maria, Luigi, and David Calderisi), Benoît Côté, Pauline Fitzgerald, Margaret Ford, Pierre Goulet, Terry Haig, Jill Harrison, André Major, Félix-Antoine Mercier, Normand Mousseau, Michael Paduano, the Poulin family (Guy, Lise-Anne, Philippe, Alexandre), Louise Rémillard, Gino Ricci, Martin Robidoux, and Nancy Turner. During the last year of the project, Inam Malik provided particular encouragement and support. And, at the University of Toronto Press, I am indebted to Jennifer DiDomenico, Robin Studniberg, Breanna Muir, and Terry Teskey for their professionalism and kindness.

The book is dedicated to my favourite teacher, who chaired the history department at Loyola College in Montreal in the 1960s, ran as a socialist (twice) in the wealthy bastion of Westmount, and introduced me to two great beacons in my life: French culture and the centuries-old struggle for social justice.

QUEBEC IN A GLOBAL LIGHT
Reaching for the Common Ground

Introduction

To the world at large, Quebec is Canada's most distinctive province. To many Canadians, it has sometimes seemed the most troublesome. But over the last quarter century, quietly but steadily, it has wrestled successfully with two of the West's most daunting challenges: protecting national values in the face of mass immigration and striking a proper balance between economic efficiency and a sound social safety net. Quebec has also taken a lead in fighting climate change. Yet, many people – including many Quebeckers – are unaware of this progress, and much remains to be done. Those achievements – and the tenacity that made them possible – are rooted in centuries of adversity and struggle.

A Sense of Destiny

Throughout their history, French Canadians have had a strong sense of destiny. But, in fact, Quebec was a pure historical accident. Named for a narrowing of the Saint Lawrence River where the French built a fortress in the early seventeenth century, neither the city nor the province was inevitable. Although the river was staring him in the face during his first voyage, Jacques Cartier did not even discover it until his second visit in 1535. And if the English explorer Henry Hudson had sailed a few years earlier than 1609 and moved further up the New York river named after him or ventured south from the great inland sea that also bears his name, New France might have become New England instead.

But if a French-speaking Quebec was an accident, its survival was not, thanks to a combination of British calculation and Gallic pride, charm, and stubbornness. That accomplishment has been central to Quebec's consciousness and culture. A beautiful expression of it is to be found in *Maria Chapdelaine*, the novel that gave several generations of school children their first image of themselves. Written by a Frenchman, Louis Hémon, and published in 1913, when the interior was still being opened up and the church and provincial government were trying to stem the loss of hundreds of thousands of people to the textile mills of New England, the book painted a portrait of a people rugged in the face of hardship. It talked of their "infinite patience," "invincible light-heartedness," and "simplicity."

The hero of the story, a stoic young woman torn between her native roots and the appeal of the modern, decides to marry a local farmer rather than follow one of her suitors to New England. Some readers have seen this as an allegory of Quebec's sad destiny: to remain *un petit peuple* (a small people). But Maria is at peace with her decision. Once it is made, she hears the "voice of Quebec" calling, half a woman singing, half a cleric preaching: "We came here three hundred years ago and stayed. Our ancestors would be proud of us because, even if we have learned very little, we have forgotten almost nothing. Strangers have come among us and taken almost all the power and money. They even call us 'backward.' But nothing has changed, and nothing will. Our duty was to preserve our culture, and we have done just that, so that perhaps a few hundred years from now, the world may still be saying: 'They're a people that don't know how to die ...'"[1]

People from other places also praised Quebec's character. In 1931, the sublime novelist of the American Midwest, Willa Cather, set her *Shadows on the Rock* in Quebec City in 1697. One of her central characters was "the free Frenchman of the great forests [with] the good manners of the Old World, the dash and daring of the New. He was proud, he was vain, he was relentless when he hated, and quickly prejudiced; but he had the old ideals of clan-loyalty, and in friendship he never counted the cost."[2]

Ten years later, in 1941, the Canadian journalist Bruce Hutchison started the long journey described in *The Unknown Country* at the village of St. Pierre, on the Ile d'Orléans, just below Quebec City. "The Frenchman has brought his humour, his cynicism, his hard realism and cheerfulness across the ocean. He has not changed much through more than three hundred years." Some considered the French Canadians a "problem" because "their [culture] is too strong to be easily absorbed in our common, tepid American sea." Occasionally, voices would complain that the English had all the power and the best jobs. "For a little while there is wild talk of an independent Quebec, a free French nation on the shores of the St. Lawrence. It is sure-fire, but never lasts. Your French Canadian is too shrewd not to know on what side his bread is buttered." He may listen to the odd nationalist. "He may cheer, and will accept a cigar or a drink on election day, but he is as canny and suspicious as a Scot."[3]

Yet, Quebeckers waited a very long time to see their culture respected in the rest of Canada. It was not until sixty years after Confederation that postage stamps were issued in English and French (1927), and Canadian banknotes were not bilingual until 1937. (To be fair, until 1925, even the province's own cheques were issued only in English.)[4] As late as 1956, a prominent Quebec journalist and future federal minister, Gérard Pelletier, walked into the Canadian High Commission on Trafalgar Square in London, speaking French, and was referred to the French Embassy.[5] And Canada was 102 years old before both languages were given equal status and French speakers had the right to receive federal services across the country in their own tongue (1969).

Self-Assertion

By then, Quebeckers had finally lost their celebrated patience. In the two centuries since the British Conquest, the *Québécois* had challenged English domination only once. That rebellion, in 1837–8, was quickly put down, its leadership was dispersed, and twelve of the rebels were hanged in Montreal. Thereafter, apart from a fit of exasperation in December 1917, when Quebec's premier Lomer Gouin allowed a debate in the legislature on whether the province should secede from Canada if the federal government persisted in conscripting young men to die on the Western Front, Quebec nationalism was confined to newspapers, lecture halls, sitting rooms, and a number of fledgling political parties.

That changed on Saturday, 20 April 1963, when the Front de libération du Québec (FLQ)* bombed an army recruiting centre in Montreal and killed the watchman, a sixty-five-year-old man named Wilfred O'Neil. A month later, they planted bombs in eleven mailboxes in the English-speaking neighbourhood of Westmount (one of which blew off the arm of the explosives expert, Walter Leja, who was trying to dismantle it). Later that day, a bomb exploded at an oil refinery at the other end of the city, blowing a hole in a one-hundred-thousand-gallon fuel tank. Police speculated that if the bomb had been placed closer to the fuel tank, hundreds might have died.[6] It was the day that Quebec – and Canada more generally – lost its innocence. Over the next seven years, the FLQ engaged in over 160 violent incidents that killed eight people and injured many more, culminating in the 1969 bombing of the Montreal Stock Exchange and the October 1970 kidnapping of a British diplomat and the murder of Quebec's deputy premier. These events – and the federal government's use of the War Measures Act to counter this European-style terrorism – shocked a society accustomed to civil debate and opposed to unnecessary squabbling (*chicanes*). They also drained support for any remaining revolutionary movement. Thereafter, nationalists pursued their cause through more conventional channels, leading to the election of the first pro-independence government on 15 November 1976.

This period of turmoil – which ushered in two decades of political uncertainty, including the 1980 referendum on independence, the 1982 patriation† of the Canadian constitution (which Quebec

---

* Quebec Liberation Front.
† "Patriation" is a Canadian neologism. The country's foundational document, the British North America Act of 1867, was a product of the British Parliament, so it could hardly be "repatriated."

refused to sign), two sets of failed constitutional negotiations in 1987 and 1992, and a second referendum in Quebec in October 1995 – sparked tensions and misunderstandings. In the rest of Canada, these events also created an image of the province as rancorous and difficult to please and, internationally, as a people struggling nobly but vainly (like the Catalans, Basques, and Scots) to reverse the tides of history.

More than twenty years after the 1995 referendum, which split the country in two emotionally and almost constitutionally as well, wounds are still healing on both sides. But much has changed. Half of Canada's population did not exist or was too young to vote in 1995, and Quebec itself has undergone profound shifts that die-hards on both sides have chosen to overlook. Like insects caught in amber, they face each other with bared mandibles, while others get on with their lives. Bitterness has given way to indifference, which in turn incubates outdated ideas of each other. The gaps in knowledge are wide and getting wider. And there are new anxieties that Canadians elsewhere – and many Quebeckers, too – have difficulty understanding. In 2016, the appointment of a Haitian-born lawyer to head Quebec's human rights commission was delayed by Opposition suggestions that she was too "multiculturalist."[7]

Purpose of This Book

But why a new book on Quebec? Most Western countries are struggling with finding a proper balance between economic efficiency and a reliable social safety net. And all multi-ethnic societies face the challenge of managing the aspirations of minority groups and protecting national cultures from the potentially distorting effects of mass immigration. While Quebec is not a paragon, it is an informative and encouraging example of how a liberal democracy has managed to handle these two sets of pressures peacefully.

Although a large number of books about Quebec are published in French each year, very few are written in English. Canada's former Commissioner of Official Languages, Graham Fraser, once said that English Canada's understanding of Quebec was always behind by a decade. Even after the Quiet Revolution of the 1960s, Quebec society continued to be seen as dominated by narrow-minded clerics, while in the 1970s a fully democratic Parti québécois was put into the same basket by outsiders as the militant and sometimes terrorist FLQ.[8] In the wake of Canada's 150th birthday and an eventful provincial election in October 2018, I believe that a frank and constructive look at Quebec society is timely. I hope this book will be revealing even for those who think they know the subject well, and that it will dispel some misconceptions, just as my research dispelled some of mine.

This book has three objectives. It will explain to outsiders as objectively as possible why many Quebeckers are still deeply concerned about their identity. It will ask young Quebeckers, particularly those who regard themselves as "progressive," to look at the long-term challenges facing the society in a new light. And it will serve as a guide for first-time visitors to the major issues facing Quebec, analysed in a wider, global context.

The book will also try to counter the prejudices of those who should know better. A Saskatchewan friend of mine who worked for thirty years at the Montreal Children's Hospital once told me that Quebec's identity concerns were "nothing that a good enema couldn't cure." Economically, he regarded the province as "the Greece of Canada." Others have tried to put themselves in Quebec's shoes. As a member of Parliament, the Liberal senator David Smith told constituents in Toronto that, if Ontario had been the only English-speaking province in the country, it would almost certainly have separated from Canada.[9]

Unlike other books on Quebec, this one will assume that the chances of Quebec's becoming independent are now extremely faint. Population changes (particularly the large number of new Quebeckers), the cosmopolitanism of young people, and the absence of any compelling practical reasons for constitutional change have rendered such debates superfluous. As a result, until recently, no prominent politician in Quebec or Ottawa was interested in reviving these issues and, where fear of a break-up once fuelled an openness to change in other parts of Canada, there is now almost total indifference to the province's special circumstances. In fact, it is doubtful that organizers could muster more than a handful of people from other provinces to rally for the federalist cause, compared with the tens of thousands who turned out in Montreal on the eve of the 1995 referendum. The October 2018 election was the first in fifty years in which independence or the possibility of another referendum was not a central issue of the campaign. Quebeckers and Canadians over fifty years of age are like married couples that have quarrelled incessantly, now relieved that the worst of the mayhem is over. Prolonged adversity has made some of them more open, attentive, and understanding; others harbour grudges that distort their thinking.

Although the battle on the Plains of Abraham lasted only fifteen minutes, its effects are still reverberating 250 years later. At the heart of Quebec society stands a stunning paradox. Home to an astonishingly creative and open-minded people, teased by some for its "cultural imperialism" in the capital of glitz, Las Vegas (Cirque du Soleil, Céline Dion), Quebec also suffers from a deep sense of isolation and insecurity. As a result, a large number of Quebeckers have not abandoned the idea of creating their own country. About a third of them – including almost half of those who speak French – still support sovereignty.[10] That is a large number of unhappy people, even if, as a nationalist politician once told me, "like Catholics, *indépendantistes* are not all practicing."[11] Indeed, various polls suggest that only half of them expect to achieve their objective.

The "Quebec Model"

This book will address two sets of questions:

Identity. How can almost half of French-speaking Quebeckers be reassured that their culture and language will be properly protected within the current political order? Or should they be encouraged to take a broader view, accept that past efforts in that direction have been largely successful, and be urged to see Quebec's situation in a more positive light? How can this identity be reconciled with a more diverse society? How solid are the foundations of Quebec's sense of fairness and solidarity?

Economy. Given Quebec's high levels of debt and taxation, what room does it have to confront the serious challenges facing the economy? How can it maintain an acceptable level of social services without continuing to shift the cost to future generations? And how can Quebec become more efficient, not just in the traditional economic sense, but also in fighting poverty and climate change?

These two themes are related, but not in the way that many people think. Critics of the independence movement once vilified it for chasing jobs, talent, and investment away to other provinces; but that argument would be hard to sustain now. Although natural resources still play a role, Quebec's economy is more varied and dynamic than it was at the time of the first wave of nationalism of the 1960s and 1970s. In 2016, the province created more jobs than all other provinces combined and Montreal's unemployment rate dropped three percentage points (to 7.3 per cent) in a single year.[12] In 2017, Quebec had the highest economic growth (3 per cent) in Canada, and that was still true through the first quarter of 2018.[13] The more direct link between identity and the economy is the pride that opinion leaders have taken in Quebec's social "model." It is in that sense – the promotion of solidarity – that identity and economy have sometimes overlapped.

Yet, many well-informed observers have questioned the merits – or at least the future – of the Quebec "model." Lucien Bouchard, who led the "Yes" forces in the 1995 referendum and was premier from 1996 to 2001, wrote in 2012:

> We always come back to the same challenge. We have to balance what is best against what is necessary. We are now at one of those moments when we need to establish a new balance. I believe that we are overly indebted and too highly taxed. Some people grind their teeth when we talk about the need to create more wealth [and hence expand the tax base]. But, if we don't, the first people to suffer will be those who benefit from an increase in government resources. In other words, we need to put as much wealth as possible at the service of social justice.[14]

Many dismiss Bouchard as a "right-winger," demonstrating how far to the left the political centre is in Quebec. As premier, he introduced subsidized childcare, equal pay for equal work, a prescriptions insurance plan, and the first public financing for the "social" economy (cooperatives, non-profits, and community self-help organizations). "No one has a monopoly on generosity," he has said. "I'm always sceptical about those who mouth nice words but are strangely silent about how they will implement their ideas."[15]

Other critics have been more biting. Éric Duhaime, a Quebec City radio commentator and economist widely dismissed as a right-wing ideologue, is as irreverent as he is incisive:

> Each day, the Quebec State collapses a little bit more before our very eyes, like the Ville-Marie tunnel that runs under the centre of Montreal. Out of shape and out of breath, it seems to be reaching the end of a cycle, with one of the heaviest debt loads in the Western world, one boy out of three dropping out of high school, an average 20-hour wait in what are still called "emergency" wards, a pension system that is running out of money, bureaucratic and trade-union practices that are preventing any kind of development, public infrastructure in disrepair, etc.[16]

Defenders of the "Quebec model" argue that, despite lower median incomes, Quebec's standard of living is higher than in Ontario, its more populous and prosperous neighbour, because of more generous social programs. Quebec, too, has been more successful in reducing the gap between rich and poor than any other part of Canada and any other country, except the Scandinavian ones. But these programs are costly, their gains are fragile, and they must be reconciled with efforts to contain the growth in public spending and create a "leaner" state.[17]

Quebec has also made major strides in trying to fight climate change – an important challenge for forward-looking economies. Public support and government-business cooperation have allowed the province to join arms with California, British Columbia, and (until recently) Ontario in trying to spur wider initiatives right across North America.*

---

* In June 2018, the new government of Ontario announced that it would be withdrawing from the carbon emissions "cap-and-trade" market. (See chapter 5.)

Personal Background

As a writer, what do I bring to these subjects? Born and educated in Quebec and the son of Italian immigrants, I experienced the challenge and pleasure of adapting to the dominant French culture. Despite my Mediterranean roots, throughout my life I have been an ardent Anglophile and Francophile in equal measure. I studied at Oxford on a Quebec Rhodes Scholarship and did postgraduate work at two other British universities. For thirty years, I shared my life with a French national and worked in a number of English- and French-speaking countries; currently, I split the year between Montreal, Paris, and New York. Between 1975 and 2002, I worked in international development, analysing strikingly different societies in Africa and Asia and advising governments on how to promote economic and social progress. Cultural and institutional factors were crucial ingredients in those assessments. Now, after spending half my life away from Quebec, I bring a detachment that allows me to see its strengths, its potential, and its drawbacks in ways that others may not.

Unfortunately, I was absent during the four most important moments of modern Quebec history: the October Crisis of 1970, the election of the first *indépendantiste* government in 1976, the May 1980 referendum (in which 60 per cent of Quebeckers rejected sovereignty), and the second referendum of October 1995 (which the nationalists lost by only 54,288 votes). Since my return to Quebec in 2002, through reading, travel, conversations, and interviews, I have tried hard to understand the significance of those events. In the process, I have delved more deeply into *indépendantiste* writings than most English-speaking Canadians would have the time and patience to do. I believe that this research, filtered through my international experience, provides a solid foundation for the essay that follows.

I should also say a word about my values. As a social democrat, I believe that the economy should serve society rather than the other way around. I am absolutely convinced of the importance of public policy but also of the power of the market to achieve some of its ends. I regard poverty as a stain on the community rather than a necessary aspect of a capitalist economy. At the same time, I think that individual effort, investment, and innovation should be rewarded. I was proud that the National Assembly voted unanimously in favour of same-sex civil unions in 2002. I cheered the 150,000 people who protested in Montreal in 2003 against the US invasion of Iraq (fifteen times larger than the turnout in Toronto, despite minus-twenty-degree weather). I was delighted by the National Assembly's eccentric (and, again, unanimous) decision in 2007 to keep the crucifix on the wall above the Speaker's chair, in deference to Quebec's heritage and defiance of the recommendation of a public commission. And I was impressed that Quebec challenged the federal government in court in 2015 to introduce assisted suicide immediately rather than wait six months for Ottawa's own guidelines to be ready. All of these events were striking reminders of the solidarity, openness, humanity, and common sense of Quebec society.

Reaching for the Common Ground

Words are especially important in Quebec, so I will avoid those that may wound readers unnecessarily. There will be no "separatists" in this book – only "nationalists," "*indépendantistes*," and "sovereignists." I will drop the jargon "francophone," "anglophone," and "allophone"* that can make debates on identity seem complicated, even anthropological. With apologies to nationalist readers, I will use the word "province" occasionally, even though some associate it with the Latin word *victus* (meaning "conquered").† Political realities and the absence of synonyms give me very little choice. While the phrases are not watertight, I will use the word "Quebeckers" most of the time

---

* Those whose first language is neither French nor English.
† At the Salon du Livre in Montreal in November 2015, the former Quebec prime minister Bernard Landry suggested that the word "province" derived from the Latin phrase *pro victus*. The Oxford English Dictionary suggests that its ultimate origins are unknown.

and "*Québécois*" only when I am referring specifically to those who have lived and worked primarily in French for several generations. Few *Québécois* use the phrase "French Canadian" to describe themselves any more, so I will avoid it almost entirely, except when I am referring to events before 1960.

The book has seven chapters. The first ("Identity") explains the origins and implications of Quebec's concern about language and culture. The second ("Diversity") describes the strains imposed on Quebec values by mass immigration. Chapter 3 ("Solidarity") offers a brief tour of the province's political culture, its progress in reducing poverty, and the state of the social safety net. That is followed by a survey of major economic challenges ("Efficiency"), one of which, climate change, is treated separately in chapter 5 ("Climate"). Chapter 6 ("Fairness") steps back and looks at the case for introducing a guaranteed annual income and proportional representation. The final chapter ("Looking Ahead") contains personal observations and recommendations for meeting the challenges set out in the book. A list of key dates and a summary of suggestions are at the end. As Quebec has not been operating in a vacuum and has consciously sought inspiration and models from other countries, each chapter will draw on international debates and data, where appropriate.

Throughout, I will try to stick to the middle ground in the belief that much more unites than divides Quebeckers. In 2005, a number of leading figures (including Lucien Bouchard) issued a manifesto entitled *Pour un Québec lucide* (For a clear-sighted Quebec), answered shortly after by a counter-manifesto, *Pour un Québec solidaire* (For a Quebec that stands together). The authors of the second tract went on to found a party by that name (Québec solidaire) that has since become one of the most lively and honourable voices in Quebec politics. With apologies to those competing visions, I hope that readers will find this book to be both *lucide* and *solidaire*.

1

Identity

A loon was laughing thinly out on the water. It was a bleak sound, reflecting John's mood almost perfectly. Late on Christmas Eve, he was breathing in the brisk sea air from a hotel balcony in Tofino, on the west coast of Vancouver Island. His wife had left him and his children had their own families to worry about. But that was not why he was feeling disconsolate. He worked in the insurance industry in Des Moines (Iowa), on the banks of a river that seventeenth-century explorers had named after Catholic "monks" for some obscure reason. (Leave it to the French to be unusual.) At the end of a busy year, he was here to reconnect with his home province and native tongue. The whole of the United States and Canada now spoke French, and British Columbia was the last pocket of the English language on the continent. Earlier, over dinner, his temper rose steadily as the restaurant played a long selection of Christmas carols almost exclusively in French. Even those originally composed in English were being played in the continent's dominant language! John was generally easy-going, but his language was dear to him and that devotion ran through his body like a steel fibre. Here, in the open air, he was trying to recover from having that fibre twanged like an electric guitar.

If English is your mother tongue – and even more so if you speak nothing else – it is hard to imagine worrying about its future. As the world's only real *lingua franca*, English is here to stay. Spoken by 1.5 billion people around the globe, it is the only successor to Esperanto – that artificial language devised to unite peoples that is now used by less than two million stout-hearted souls. Pedants may worry about the gradual disappearance of the English subjunctive or the impoverishment of the common vocabulary, but that is like complaining about clouds obscuring parts of the Rockies. The mountain range remains impressive and unshakeable.

Large countries, like China, Brazil, Russia, and Indonesia, are culturally secure. Spanish, Arabic, Portuguese, and French are spoken by hundreds of millions of people and are the national languages of more than one country.[1] Even Italian, which is hardly spoken outside its motherland and diaspora, remains strong for historical and geographical reasons, and perhaps also because of the Italians' resistance to learning other people's languages. But small countries like the Netherlands and Croatia have trouble shutting themselves off so easily.

In fact, small cultures everywhere face a steamroller. Every two weeks, one of the world's seven thousand languages dies; in fact, half of them may be extinct by the end of the century.[2] For example, only three of Canada's fifty-three native languages (Inuit, Cree, and Algonquin) are expected to survive. In isolated places like the truncated highlands of New Guinea, languages are particularly at risk; but even international ones spoken in geographical pockets can falter. To the *Québécois*, the corruption and virtual disappearance of French in the southern US state of Louisiana (a patois known as Cajun, from the original "*Acadien*," or Acadian) is the most sobering example.

Language and Identity

But why is language central to some people's sense of identity? In the words of the Canadian Mohawk artist and activist, Ellen Gabriel Katsi' Tsakwas, "Language is a gift from our ancestors and a link with our cosmology. It helps us understand our place in the world and refreshes our connection with Mother Earth and other living creatures from one generation to the next. Language and culture, like social and economic development, are inseparable parts of achieving full human rights and self-determination."[3]

Words like "cosmology" may seem inflated to Anglo-Saxon ears. And what does English, French, or Cree have to do with our relationship to other creatures? But being open to these ideas and concerns is crucial to understanding why small, vulnerable cultures worry about their future. For them, a dying language is not a quaint and dispensable thread in a global tapestry but a particular way of looking at the world and a treasury of stories, knowledge, and wisdom. Quebec nationalists can sound as deep as any poet of the First Nations on the subject. In the words of one recent writer, "Losing one's language is not about beginning a new life in North America and learning another. Every immigrant is capable of that. Losing one's language is the same as losing one's soul and letting the souls of one's ancestors wander aimlessly in a void."[4]

"The French language," writes Denise Bombardier, a prominent Quebec journalist and novelist,

> is our river leading to the sea, or the outside world. It is less a tool of communication than a carrier of our emotions, ideas, reactions, reality. Thanks to it, the *Québécois* inherit a glorious and prestigious past. From Diderot to Stendhal, Voltaire to Camus, Montesquieu to Maupassant and Proust, French writers belong entirely to us. The French language distinguishes us but it also isolates us and that isolation stimulates our creativity. Our writers, playwrights, and actors draw on this language that crossed the ocean and evolved over several centuries, fortifying itself and affirming itself differently than in the mother country.[5]

Language, of course, is not central to everyone's identity. People living in the middle of Michigan or Saskatchewan or large parts of China will not think of themselves in linguistic terms, unless they are members of a cultural minority. There are better ways of distinguishing themselves. The Nobel Prize–winning economist Amartya Sen describes himself as an Asian, an Indian citizen, a Bengali, a resident of the United States and the United Kingdom, a dabbler in philosophy, a Sanskritist, a strong believer in secularism and democracy, a man, a feminist, a heterosexual, a defender of gay and lesbian rights, a non-Brahmin from a Hindu background, and at the same time a non-believer.[6] He is also a vegetarian, tennis fan, lover of poetry, environmental activist, theatre-goer, and jazz enthusiast. Our shared humanity, he feels, is "miniaturized" when the many things that distinguish us as individuals are reduced to a single classification, such as religion, community, culture, or nation.[7] He could have added language to that list.

Another Indian writer, Salman Rushdie, relishes "hybridity, impurity, intermingling, the transformation that comes of new and unexpected combinations of human beings, cultures, ideas, politics, movies, songs."[8] Rushdie had good reason to prefer such a muddle to purism and fundamentalism, as a religious death-order hung over him for writing irreverently about Islam. But not everyone wants to become a mongrel. For reasons of security, a sense of order, tradition, family loyalty, respect for history, or simple religious faith, many people prefer to identify themselves rather narrowly, and some Quebeckers are no exception.

Language becomes a more natural defining mark in pluralist societies where a cultural minority no longer feels protected by geography, history, or legislation. Think of LGBTQ people pressed by a history of fear and discrimination into believing that their sexual identity is the most important thing about them, even though for most human beings sex is a necessary, pleasant, but generally occasional pastime.

Language in Quebec

Nationalist impatience in Quebec draws on a long record of threats and insults to their language. Two recent writers have listed thirty episodes in Canadian history that were a direct threat to the survival of French, including now-distant controversies about limiting the teaching of the language in New Brunswick (1871), Prince Edward Island (1877), Manitoba (1890), Alberta (1905), and Ontario (1912).[9]

The fable at the beginning of this chapter was inspired by an opinion piece in the Montreal newspaper *Le Devoir* in

January 2008. The setting was different, with the visitor staying at a hotel in the Charlevoix Region, overlooking the Saint Lawrence River. He had tried to make allowances for the fact that some of the guests at the hotel might be English speaking and he hoped that things would improve by New Year's Eve. Instead, at the stroke of midnight, in the opening moments of the four hundredth anniversary of the founding of Quebec, a young *Québécoise* sang – in English. "What has become of our artists?" he lamented. "Where are the Leclercs, the Vigneaults, the Charlebois, the Dubois, the Dufresnes, and the Ferlands [all famous Quebec singers], who carried our language forward and made a good living doing it?" He was not opposed to foreign languages. Quite the contrary. "But the time has come to decide. Rather than betray our own language, why not move consciously on to something else? Instead of agonizing about this for several more generations, as our cousins in the rest of North America have done, why not establish a new political party with the sole purpose of anglicising us all in just 10–15 years?"[10]

French is still a major world language. But, unlike France or French-speaking African countries that share borders and an interest in preserving their language, Quebec is physically isolated, stuck between the harsh North, the blustery Atlantic, and a sea of more than three hundred million English-speaking people to the west and south of them. That said, they are not the only people with a sense of history, vulnerability, and almost religious attachment to their tongue.

In surlier moments, in the 1970s and 1980s, Quebec nationalists compared the English-speaking minority to the white Rhodesians or South Africans of that time who were resisting majority rule. But the parallel was inexact. In fact, it is the French Canadians who resemble the Afrikaners, descendants of seventeenth-century Dutch settlers, who are obsessed with the survival of their culture in a sea of Others, fighting fossilization and irrelevance. Having evolved in relative isolation, their language is barely understood in the Netherlands today. Yet, to Afrikaners, it is the key to their identity, rooted in a strong religious faith (Calvinist, not Catholic) and simple rural values, both of which are now on the wane.

In Bloemfontein, there is a Museum of Afrikaans Literature, and near Paarl, on a hill overlooking the Stellenbosch winelands, there is something even more remarkable: a monument to the Afrikaans language, reflecting a mixture of pride and anxiety. Stark and impressively modern, given its nostalgic purpose, it was erected in 1975 on the one hundredth anniversary of standardizing the language. As you reach the top of the steps to the esplanade, which commands a view of the surrounding countryside, a grim message greets you, engraved in the final step in Afrikaans: "This is our concern." When I visited the place, my guide told me that some black nationalists wanted the monument demolished, as a symbol of past tyranny. Though he was of mixed race and had been forced to learn Afrikaans at school despite speaking English at home, the guide thought this wrongheaded. "It's only a language, but people who have spoken it all their lives revere it and are worried about its future."[11] This was obvious to a Quebecker, but I was impressed to hear someone from a once-oppressed minority speak up for the culture of his former masters. I was also relieved that we had not yet felt obliged to erect a monument to French in Quebec.

When he visited Quebec in 1907, the English writer Rudyard Kipling was also struck by the parallel with Dutch-English relations in South Africa: "Have you ever noticed that Canada has to deal in the lump with most of the problems that affect us others, severally? For example, she has the Double-Language, Double-Law, Double-Politics drawback in a worse form than South Africa, because, unlike our Dutch, her French cannot well marry outside their religion, and they take their orders from Italy [the Vatican] – less central than Pretoria or Stellenbosch [important Afrikaner towns]."[12]

The Survival of French in Quebec

How did the French language survive and even thrive in a potentially hostile environment? One explanation is the late emergence of Quebec as a modern economy. Another was the constant threat to their culture by "strangers" and the need to resist perceived oppression. A third influence was the role of the Catholic Church, which tied its interests to the nationalist cause. But the main reason was sheer stubbornness. Against all odds, ignoring fashion and reason, undaunted by the greatest cultural power in human history next door (the United States), and seemingly strengthened by the very improbability of their cause, the *Québécois* have remained faithful to their origins.

Historical factors also played a role. As in other parts of the world, the record of colonialism was not all negative. The future of French Canada was actually protected by the British Parliament in the Quebec Act of 1774, which guaranteed freedom of language and religion and the preservation of French civil law. This was not a concession to common sense or "human rights," but an effort to head off possible French Canadian support for the American Revolution. As a result, even though the Americans occupied Montreal during the winter of 1775–6, they made little progress in expanding their foothold and were forced to retreat after their general, Richard Montgomery, was killed in the attack on Quebec City. Thereafter, it was French Canadian willpower, not British paternalism or open-mindedness, that kept French Canada French.

Once the American Revolution was over, there were several attempts to roll back the protections of the Quebec Act. Already, during the original debate in the British House of Commons, one of the greatest orators of the day, Edmund Burke, opposed the legislation on the grounds that it would preserve the *Canadiens'* "old prejudices (and) their old customs" and would effectively reconstitute New France, "the only difference [being that] they will have George III for Louis XVI."[13] In 1822, a bill to unite Upper and Lower Canada and abolish French as an official language was dropped after protests in both Canadas.[14] In 1839, the British governor-general, Lord Durham, recommended assimilating the French Canadians, a people "with no history and no literature," into English-speaking North America. The Act of Union of 1840 specified that English would be the only official language of the new legislature, but in 1843 a different governor-general encouraged London to recognize the official status of French.[15]

The *Canadiens* used every tool at their disposal to protect their tongue – including flattery. Defending his right to propose bills in the legislature in his own language, the marquis Alain Chartier de Lotbinière insisted in January 1793 that all his countrymen were loyal to their new sovereign, George III: "Hearing French in the mouths of his new subjects is bound to please him because it will remind him of the glory of his Empire and the fact that the peoples of this vast continent were British in their hearts even before they were able to pronounce a single word of English."[16] Referring to the American invasion of 1775, de Lotbinière continued: "This city, these walls, this very Chamber were saved in part by the zeal and courage of my compatriots against attacks from people who spoke very good English."[17]

French-English Rivalry

That there have been long-simmering tensions between the French and English in Quebec is hardly surprising, as they are heirs to one of the most ancient enmities in history. No other two nations fought a Hundred Years War (1337–1453) and then came back for more. It was during the "second" hundred years war (1688–1815) that New France fell to the English.[18] The people of St. Malo, the stone-girded town on the coast of Brittany that was the birthplace of Canada's "discoverer" Jacques Cartier, still boast that they were never taken by the English. When they head off on holiday, they turn their backs on England and drive east or south. The English Channel is so narrow that determined people have swum across it. But even in an age of globalization, the two peoples remain profoundly different. I once met a senior government official in London who travelled regularly to places like New Delhi and Buenos Aires but considered his most exotic journey to be the short train ride to Paris.

Remarkably, this rivalry never seems to run out of steam. In March 2003, when British prime minister Tony Blair was trying to persuade his Labour MPs to back the invasion of Iraq, his accounts of "duplicitous" French diplomacy at the UN proved so upsetting that some joked it would have been easier to declare war on France.[19] At about the same time, Chris Patten, the European Union's "foreign minister," referred to a colleague in Brussels as "the sort of Frenchman whom we British need to exist so that we can recall occasionally how wonderfully generous we were to sign the Entente Cordiale."[20] A recent history has even documented France's "secret wars" with the Anglo-Saxons in Africa and Latin America over the last seventy years and quotes Charles de Gaulle confiding to a friend, "We're going to take back from the English all they stole from us: first Quebec, then Mauritius and then the Anglo-Norman [Channel] Islands."[21]

Like all strong cultures, France and England are proud of their histories. They make few excuses for themselves and treasure the traces of past successes. Every day, Londoners wander through Trafalgar Square and Waterloo Station (named after famous victories against the French) while Parisians whiz through Metro stations named Austerlitz, Iéna, and Pyramides (triumphs against the Prussians, Austrians, and Egyptians, as the French rarely defeated the English). The French may be more boastful, but they have a great deal to crow about. Both countries think they civilized the rest of the world. Each "invented" civil liberties: the English at Runnymede in 1215 during the face-off between King John and his nobles; the French in 1789, at the start of their revolution.

But the two cultures will often respect each other. There may be more Francophile Britons than French Anglophiles, but French intellectuals since Voltaire (1694–1778) have grudgingly admired English institutions and *sang-froid*. Some French would like their politics to be less ideological, while some English would prefer their government to be more principled. A Frenchman will admire English calm just as much as an English woman will appreciate the expressiveness of her opposite number. But language divides them more deeply than the Channel, with the French more sensitive about it, as they appear to be on the losing side in the international marketplace. The French are scrupulous about their tongue, correcting foreigners constantly; the English are more forgiving, which is one of the reasons English will remain the language spoken by most Eurocrats even after Brexit. But one has to admire the persistence with which the French defend their tongue, revering it like a monument and caressing it like a lover.

Sometimes, like quicksilver, national traits can be difficult to pin down. In late 1893, a French Canadian tried to blow up Nelson's Column in Montreal, provoking an editorial in *The London Spectator*. Oddly enough, the writer did not rush to the defence of the Hero of Trafalgar. Thinking of the admiral's extramarital affairs, the paper admitted that Nelson was not a moral man. But that was hardly a reason for blowing up his monument. "Nelson was a highly-strung, very sensitive, and rather vainglorious man, more like a well-trained Frenchman than an Englishman." He won victories for England, the editorial concluded, and that was why he was attacked in Montreal.[22]

All the same, some French and English people seem to inhabit different universes. The best-selling popular historian Paul Johnson once described Charles de Gaulle, president of France (1958–69), "as an egoist on a superhuman scale [embodying] the natural selfishness which is the salient characteristic of France and of French people generally."[23] The man who complained about hearing Christmas carols in a "foreign language" on the banks of the Saint Lawrence conceded that English is more suited to "our modern values: power, money, and war."[24] With opinions like these, it is hardly surprising that French and English speakers in Canada continue to have their differences.

"Double Inspiration"

Fortunately, a frontier history, the egalitarian example of the United States, and decades of adversity have worn away the sharp edges of that conflict in Quebec. There is less arrogance and more even-handedness than you will find in the two mother countries. Most Quebeckers (like most Canadians) are in fact American in the broad sense of the word. They are direct, unpretentious, fair-minded, and ambitious, but willing to give others a chance. Except for highly visible religious jewellery or clothing, most Quebeckers are willing to overlook differences in national origins and beliefs. Regional accents are a badge of honour rather than an obstacle to success.

The other redeeming feature is that Quebeckers are in fact a product of the two cultures. The Conquest was double-edged. While the British were the victors at the start, their descendants absorbed the values of the society they had taken over.[25] As time wore on, the merging of tastes and outlooks grew more striking. The novelist Gabrielle Roy (1909–83), who was originally from southern Manitoba, was astounded by how familiar London seemed, the first time she visited. It was when she arrived in France that she felt in a foreign land. The journalist Denise Bombardier had the same experience when she dropped in to a pastry shop in Oxford and discovered all the cakes she had grown up with in Montreal, including cream puffs, which – strangely enough – she preferred to their French rivals.[26] Politicians like Pierre Elliott Trudeau, Jacques Parizeau, and Pierre Bourgault studied in the United Kingdom and spoke English with a precision and timbre that could put English Canadians to shame.

Some French Canadians, notably church leaders, regarded the Conquest as doubly providential, preserving Quebec from the terrors of the French Revolution and the "errors" of the American one. The auxiliary bishop of Quebec City, Monsignor Joseph-Octave Plessis, welcomed the British defeat of Napoleon's navy off the Egyptian coast in 1799: "We should be deeply grateful to the British for all they have done for us, including protecting our very faith, and realize that our happiness is closely bound up with theirs."[27]

What would have become of Quebec, asks Alain Dubuc, journalist for the Montreal paper La Presse, without the English Conquest? It was already a colony, albeit a French one. Would it have revolted against the French crown like the Americans against the English one? Been taken over by the Americans? Sold to them, like Louisiana? Or become a troubled overseas territory like Martinique or Guadeloupe? "Our culture is the product of that encounter. A French past seeded with English political traditions, a cuisine which is often more English than French (like shepherd's pie), and folk music and dance that is largely Irish and Scottish. What makes our society unique is this blending of influences. We are hybrids. Once the French of North America, we have become North Americans who speak French."[28]

In the view of the contemporary historian Jocelyn Létourneau, there is much to be said for thinking of Quebec as a society of "double inspiration." "Unable to ignore or understand each other, and having to get along despite their differences, the two groups have formed a society that is both multi-coloured and discordant, incomplete and fully-developed, disconnected but fitted together."[29] Quebeckers are accustomed to ambiguity and have generally preferred negotiation and reconciliation to violence. Even the 1837–8 rebellion, he says, was more improvised than planned and not supported by the general population. Since then, Quebeckers have been comfortable with complicated solutions.[30]

Quebec intellectuals ask questions out loud that other Canadians consider in the privacy of philosophy courses or church. How can we remain open to others and still be true to ourselves? How can we build a healthy future while respecting our history and traditions? Some want to hang on to the "timeless" elements of Quebec's personality, worrying about the "trap" of multiculturalism and fashionable talk about the diminishing importance of national identities. Others want to revitalize Quebec's self-image. The first defend a fortress under siege: the second believe that Quebec can best face contemporary challenges by being open and hospitable to cultural differences.[31]

Létourneau prefers the middle ground, believing that personal moorings are important in dealing with others but that identity is constantly being remoulded through engagement with others. "Certainly, we shouldn't say that Quebec is a model of how to live together. It has its share of problems. But, contrary to the claims of the alarmists, Quebec is not on the verge of anarchy or disintegration. Its culture – or, to be more precise, its cultures – are vibrant and have never resounded more loudly, even internationally. Though some people express themselves strongly, there is no real issue of social cohesion in Quebec."[32]

Fifty Years of Introspection

Most Quebeckers would probably agree with that assessment. But arriving there has been a tortuous struggle. In the fifty years leading up to the 1995 referendum, Quebec thinkers analysed their history and character almost to death. And a recurring element was a remarkable degree of self-hatred. In a cascade of works, writers portrayed a society still bearing the scars of a troubled childhood. Historians at the University of Montreal argued that Quebeckers had never really recovered from the British Conquest, an "apocalyptic trauma" that tore the "young colony out of its protective, nurturing environment, impaired its organization as a society, and condemned it to political and economic subordination."[33]

Unlike their counterparts at Laval University in Quebec City, who thought the *Québécois* were largely responsible for their own cultural, economic, and political condition, the Montreal school blamed the English conquerors and their still-domineering descendants. All the *Québécois* could hope for, they said, was to resist assimilation as long as possible. Unsurprisingly, some scholars have referred to this group as "melancholy."

Hubert Aquin (1929–77) talked about the "cultural fatigue" of his contemporaries: their masochism and sense of unworthiness, depression, lack of vigour, torn between suicide and self-assertion; in short, their "difficulty of being" (*difficulté d'être*).[34] It didn't help that the *Canadiens* had been not only conquered by the English but also abandoned by their "mother," France. At the Treaty of Paris, which ended the Seven Years War (1756–63), France chose to keep the West Indian sugar island of Guadeloupe instead of Canada, which it saw as too expensive to administer. How free that choice was is a matter of speculation. After all, as the main victor in the worldwide conflict, the British wanted to retain French Canada for strategic reasons.

For those who still regarded Quebec as a colony, the wave of "self-determination" sweeping across Asia and Africa at the time was a challenge and inspiration. Quebec writers drew on the existentialism of Jean-Paul Sartre and Albert Camus and the Marxist anti-colonialism of Frantz Fanon, both coming to a boil in the Paris of the 1950s and 1960s. They accused the English of being subtle rather than brutal, craftily shaping the French Canadian self-image into one of personal inadequacy and guilt instead of "normal" resentment towards their masters. André D'Allemagne (1929–2001) referred to a "never-ending genocide" and suggested that Québécois cowardice, conservatism, self-absorption, and xenophobia were all the direct results of their mental colonization. Pierre Vallières (1938–98) called them the "white niggers of North America" and insisted on overthrowing capitalism before worrying about political independence. "One flag more or less will not disturb the universal system of exploiting natural resources and cheap labour."[35]

For Fernand Dumont (1927–97), sociologist, philosopher, theologian, and poet, the Québécois had taken their cue from the conqueror's assessment of them, which varied "between pity for our backwardness and tenderness for our folkloric ways." Quebec's chronic sense of inferiority explained why it had trouble confronting other cultures. He hoped that political independence would change this, but he was not sure. "There are peoples who can look back to some great founding action: a revolution, a declaration of independence, a heroic event that inspires grandeur. In the origins of Quebec society, there was no such thing: only an enduring resistance."[36] One has to wonder whether this depressing line of analysis wasn't a greater factor in subduing the self-esteem of French Canadians than the Conquest itself.

The Laval school has been more positive and less given to psychoanalytic language. Guy Laforest, a political scientist who voted "Yes" in the 1995 referendum, objects to the notion that independence is "a necessary transition from acne-ridden, tormented adolescence to the serene maturity of adulthood."[37] "Wishing Quebec to get over the Conquest is not the same as acting as if it never happened. Getting over it means accepting that Quebec is distinct but also pluralist; that the institutions of British parliamentarianism belong to us as much as to anyone else; and that, yes, French should be our common language, but that English is also part of our history. In a word, it means accepting that Quebec is a hybrid."[38]

Yet, the "melancholy" school is still very much alive. In 2015 a father-and-son team, Roger and Jean-François Payette, published *Une fabrique de servitude* (Factory of servitude), in which they argued that Quebec culture (poetry, novels, plays, TV) has conditioned the *Québécois* to be passive, to avoid friction and argument, and to lose interest in controlling their own future. For them, even the political watershed of the 1960s is fondly remembered for being "Quiet" rather than a real "Revolution." For the Payettes, the *Québécois* are like adolescents, more interested in immediate pleasures than taking responsibility for their lives.[39] The labour lawyer and writer Pierre Vadeboncoeur has complained that "we prefer to submit and adapt to history, rather than create it."[40]

Sympathizers outside Quebec frown on such analyses. "The genius of our politics [lies] in the fact that we [have] never imposed a single national identity on anyone," says Michael Ignatieff, an international specialist in politics and human rights and (for two unhappy years) leader of the federal Liberal Party. "What I rejected about separatism was not the pride in nationhood but the insistence on a state, the belief that Quebeckers must make an existential choice between Quebec and Canada ... [Most] Quebeckers wanted to be Quebeckers and Canadians in whatever order they believed right. It was kind of a moral tyranny on the part of the separatists to force them to choose between parts of their own selves."[41]

Complex Heritage

A major reason for such "moral tyranny" is that, in Quebec, history is never very far away and remains an inflammatory subject. In 2009, neither the federal nor provincial government organized events to mark the 250th anniversary of the 1759 battle that transformed North America. The feeling on both sides was that it could not be commemorated, let alone "celebrated," safely. Perhaps fortunately, the 400th anniversary of Quebec City the year before had consumed a great deal of energy and money. Somehow, the establishment of a French presence on the continent was a safer, more uplifting event to remember. Even then, many nationalists hung their heads that the Saint Jean-Baptiste Day concert that year featured the British singer Paul McCartney entertaining a rapturous crowd of one hundred thousand young people – in English – on the very battlefield where the British had beaten the French.

The historian Jocelyn Létourneau is not given to flamboyant phrases, but he is almost savage in describing the sacredness of 1759: "It is no common event. It is something precious that you have to venerate blindly and kiss like a relic, because its cult protects you from the demons of losing your identity and being unfaithful to the motherland."[42] Yet, earlier generations made their peace with the event, with the two generals of the day locked in a posthumous embrace that would have surprised them both. While 13 September 1759 proved to be the decisive battle, the Conquest was not complete until the capitulation of Montreal a year later. In between, French and *Canadien* forces overwhelmed the British at Sainte-Foy on 28 April 1760 but could not press their advantage before British reinforcements arrived in the Saint Lawrence. Ninety-five years later, a future premier of Quebec, Pierre-Joseph-Olivier Chauveau, unveiled a monument to the three thousand men who died there, wondering, "If they could see this countryside as rich and happy as it was devastated then; our city, once ruined, now flourishing in the arts of peace; and, above all, our French language spoken over their tombs, with our religion and nationality intact under an English domination they feared so much, might they not want to return for a while?"[43]

On Dufferin Terrace, not far from the Plains of Abraham, there is a large stone column commemorating both Wolfe and Montcalm, which is the only joint memorial on earth to the winner and loser of the same battle. In Montreal, two grimy streets named after them run parallel to each other, cutting through the Gay Village. In the past, Canadians and Quebeckers took pride in these signs of equanimity and level-headedness. However, Camille Laurin, an influential minister of culture, the "father" of the controversial 1977 language law, and a professional psychiatrist, regarded all of this as a symptom of Quebeckers' "schizophrenia."[44]

Yet, the traces of Quebec's complex heritage are visible everywhere. Many nationalists are now secular and republican; yet no one has suggested removing the white cross and Bourbon *fleur de lys* from the provincial flag. Montreal's emblem gives equal importance to its four founding peoples: the French lily, the English rose, the Irish shamrock, and the Scottish thistle.* There is even a debate about the origins of the phrase on Quebec licence plates, *Je me souviens* (I remember). Introduced by the first *indépendantiste* government in 1978 to replace *La Belle Province* (the beautiful province), a reminder of Quebec's subservient status, the new motto was not necessarily a reference to the long history of French Canadian suffering. Some have argued that the words, copied from the façade of the National Assembly, were placed there by its architect to celebrate Quebec's bicultural origins. According to this version of events, they were the first words of a poem he may have composed himself: "I remember that I was born under the [French] lily but raised under the [English] rose."[45]

The public is now more relaxed about the past than many opinion-makers. Young *Québécois*, in particular, are much more comfortable with English as a language and the "English" as an ethnic community than their parents were. And according to a survey funded by the 2007–8 Bouchard-Taylor Commission, 80 per cent of French speakers agree that the English "co-founded" their society.[46]

But nationalists tend to know their history better than anyone else, and many still feel the sores of past disappointments very deeply. According to Michel Arseneault, a journalist with the Quebec weekly newsmagazine *L'Actualité* and Radio France Internationale, "The trouble with many of us is that we look at our situation from too close up. If we compare our history with that of the entire British Empire, Quebeckers have not done all that badly. But it's true that pulling our fat out of the fire [*tirer notre épingle du jeu*] is not quite as satisfying psychologically as killing our father."[47]

---

* In September 2017, in an elegant nod to the First Nations, the City of Montreal added a white pine (a tree species native to Eastern Canada) to the centre of the flag.

Far from being a minority forced to languish on the margins of power, for four decades (from April 1968 to April 2008), Quebeckers were prime minister of Canada for more than thirty-six years. The current prime minister is also a Quebecker. French president François Mitterand (1981–95) once admitted to being perplexed about Quebec's restlessness when he heard that Canada's governor general, prime minister, head of the armed forces, chief justice of the Supreme Court, and speaker of the House of Commons were all French speaking.[48]

Cultural Insecurity

Such facts, however, are immaterial to those convinced that their language is dying out. One recent study predicts that the French-speaking population of Quebec will drop from 82 per cent to 75 per cent during the next forty years.[49] Given the challenges the language will face, that number seems reassuringly high. But the situation in Montreal is more worrisome, with native French speakers likely to drop from 52 per cent to 42 per cent during the same period. Already, more than 20 per cent of immigrants (about two hundred thousand people) do not speak French, with Latin Americans and Arabs doing better than the Chinese, Indians, and Filipinos. Only two-thirds of Montrealers now work in French. One reason is that 60 per cent of immigrant adults refuse to take government-sponsored French courses, up from 40 per cent in 2008. Granted, a large number of immigrants (40 per cent) now come from French-speaking countries (France, the Maghreb, West Africa, Haiti). But another more troubling explanation is that many immigrants can now work and live in the Greater Montreal region without knowing French.[50] Yet, 85 per cent of Quebeckers still speak French primarily and 94.5 per cent of them are able to conduct a conversation in the language.[51]

Another possibility is that the government's willingness to provide services in English has undercut the need for greater integration by new Quebeckers. In the 1970s and 1980s, many Canadians criticized Quebec's introduction of unilingualism (French) at the very time that the federal government was implementing bilingualism (English and French). But, even under *indépendantiste* governments, every Quebec citizen has had the right to apply for a driver's licence, obtain a health card, fill in tax forms, register a business, and receive medical care in English – which is more than can be said for French speakers in Canada's other provinces. To English Quebeckers, this only seems fair; but to those worried about the future of French, it may help to explain the overall decline in the number of Quebeckers using French.

Threats to Quebec culture are a fixture in the media, with undercover reporters trying to ferret out discomforting facts. Some years ago, the Montreal tabloid *Journal de Montréal* sent one of its stringers to ninety-five local businesses and convinced fifteen of them to hire him even though he claimed to speak no French. The good news – that 85 per cent of them said no – was turned on its head and the paper spoke of the "threat" to French-speaking consumers.[52]

It must be said that extremists in the English community offer constant fuel for the insecure nationalist. Five years ago, I had dinner with a senior executive from Bell Canada, whose headquarters are in Montreal. A native of Alberta, he had been living in Quebec for eight years and had made absolutely no effort to learn French. Even worse, he liked to bait taxi drivers by asking them to drive him home to "Nun's Island" (the old English name for *Île des Sœurs*). Very few drivers knew what he was talking about. Instead of letting them off the hook, he would jump into a different taxi, feeling triumphant. I remember hoping that he took a very long time to get home each night. I also knew that if he had worked in Poland for eight years he would have learned Polish.

Because of their cultural insecurity, when criticized, Quebeckers can be extremely prickly. In March 2017, an article in the national newsmagazine *Maclean's* suggested that the failure to rescue motorists trapped overnight in their cars on a major highway during a snowstorm reflected a collapse in social values rather than just oversights at the Department of Transport. The hubbub that followed forced McGill University to disavow the article's contents (the author was a McGill employee). A retired judge, writing in the French-language newspaper *Le Devoir*, compared the article to the calumnies that provoked the genocide of eight hundred thousand people in Rwanda in 1994. Within a day, the author himself apologized abjectly for his "errors" and "exaggerations" and resigned his position at the university. Even Quebec's premier said he was astonished that McGill could employ someone who paraded his "prejudices" in public.[53] (Imagine the governor of California reacting to an isolated article on the state of the Californian soul.)

The same day the *Maclean's* piece appeared, a much more insulting article was published in the French-language tabloid *Le Journal de Montréal*: "Quebec is going down, and nobody gives a damn, as long as convenience stores can sell beer 24 hours a day. Look around the place. Their old people steep in their own shit, they can't even manage a snowstorm, and civil servants are paid to do nothing. Quebec is the paradise of comics and caricaturists. The place is a bloody mess but, boy, do they ever laugh. Their province is officially the poorest in the country and their debt is $280 billion. But so what? As long as the *Canadiens* [Montreal's ice hockey team] make the playoffs, everything's okay."[54]

Yet, the article barely drew a comment, except a rather sobering one from Don McPherson of the *Montreal Gazette*, one of Quebec's foremost English-language political commentators. The first writer, he pointed out, was English speaking and published his piece in a magazine based outside Quebec. The second wrote in French and was well known for his irritating views, like a tedious uncle at family gatherings. "For to belong to the English-speaking community in Quebec is to be excluded from the French-speaking one, the true *Québécois* nation. And, every now and then, it's useful to be reminded of that."[55]

Lingering Sores

Although Canada is formally bilingual, it is nothing of the sort. The Danes and the Dutch use two languages (including English) more often than most Canadians. Except in parts of Ontario,

Manitoba, and the Atlantic provinces, where there is a sizeable number of French speakers, the only place where the two dominant cultures co-exist is Quebec and, even then, that is only strictly true in Montreal. The rest of Canada and Quebec go their separate ways. Pierre Fortin, a former head of the Canadian Economics Association, travelled on business to Ottawa five to six times a year for forty-five years and was never able to find a taxi driver who spoke French in the capital of an officially bilingual country.[56]

Even in Montreal, the word "co-exist" ignores a gulf that never seems to narrow. The "two solitudes" – coined by Hugh McLennan in his 1945 novel of that name – have never been bridged. Denise Bombardier is walking proof of that: "Although I was the anchor of public affairs programs on French-language TV for more than thirty years, interviewing all the key political and cultural actors of the day, no one recognizes me in English Montreal. In the rest of the province, I feel like part of the family."[57]

Though still a nationalist, she challenges extreme depictions of the past. "Like the climate they live in, Quebeckers can be excessive, turning their history into theatre."[58] But she is wary of multiculturalism, where "nothing exists except a collection of minorities of different languages, cultures, and traditions, with English as their common means of communication." Fortunately, she thinks, there will always be enough "intolerant' and "nostalgic" people to stand up to globalization.[59]

But globalization has not been the only threat to Quebec. A large part of Quebec's mood springs from the venom with which much of Canada has reacted to its aspirations. Some of her own native sons (Pierre Trudeau, Jean Chrétien, Stéphane Dion) were seen as appealing to redneck opinion elsewhere in Canada that wanted to "put Quebec in its place," rather than drawing on the best in everyone to build a stronger national community. Some opposition to past constitutional proposals was based on genuine anxiety about going too far to accommodate one province and having the entire federation unravel as a result. But much of it, too, appeared to come from pure anger at the idea that any province should regard itself as unique. While Trudeau's opposition to Quebec's "special status" was a thoroughly rational position for a constitutional lawyer, it became an obsession that ignored the emotional and cultural energies that were surging in the province. It also appeared to contradict other positions Trudeau had taken in the past.

His nemesis, the leading *indépendantiste* politician René Lévesque, quoted Trudeau describing the French Canadians in 1956 as a people who were "defeated, occupied, decapitated, ousted from commerce, driven back from the towns, reduced little by little to a minority position and diminished in influence in a country they themselves had discovered, explored, and colonized."[60] Trudeau had also praised the Judicial Committee of the Privy Council in London for decisions in favour of devolving greater powers to the provinces. "If the law lords had not moved in this direction," he wrote in 1964, "Quebec separation might not be a threat today; it might be an accomplished fact."[61] During the 1980s and 1990s, enlightened federalists like the Conservative prime minister Brian Mulroney and Ontario's socialist premier Bob Rae tried to save something from the rubble of thirty years of bickering by backing various constitutional reforms. Yet, even in retirement, Trudeau fought back.

Few people outside Quebec can imagine how deeply wounding it was for Quebeckers in 1982 to have two of their very own (Trudeau and Chrétien) write the province out of the new Canadian constitution by agreeing to an amending formula without Quebec's consent. It didn't help that this was done by the country's other provincial leaders behind Lévesque's back in what became known as "The Night of the Long Knives." As one of Canada's two founding peoples, the *Québécois* felt thoroughly entitled to their right to veto any major changes of that kind, and any other outcome was simply unthinkable to them.* Later efforts to repair the damage caused more bad blood rather than less. When the proposed Meech Lake constitutional formula

---

* Representatives of Canada's First Peoples sometimes claim that they also "founded" the country, but in concrete terms their role was limited and involuntary. That said, without their military support, the *Canadiens* might have been beaten by the English early on and been incorporated into the American colonies.

collapsed, the province's world-renowned philosopher Charles Taylor declared: "On 23 June 1990, the 1867 Constitution died morally in Quebec."[62] And, in the months that followed, support for independence in Quebec surged to 61 per cent.*

That set in train the march towards a second referendum on independence in October 1995. One of the leaders of the Yes campaign, the *wunderkind* head of the Action démocratique du Québec, Mario Dumont, was nervous that day: "I was only twenty-five years old. While I was aware of its importance and the stakes involved, seeing it portrayed as the biggest international news item drove it home to me. My legs were shaking when I headed for the shower that morning."[63] Despite nationalist claims that French speakers have always been "afraid to be free," the majority of *Québécois* took the leap that day. According to Bernard Landry, a former Quebec premier (2001–3), his predecessor Jacques Parizeau was wrong in blaming the "ethnic vote" for the narrow defeat that day. "If more people in Quebec City had voted Yes," Landry told me, "it would have passed. People in Shawinigan (Chrétien's riding) voted Yes. So did the people of Sherbrooke (Charest's riding).† People in the National Capital [Quebec City] were just a little older and hence more risk-averse than the rest of the *Québécois*."[64]

Many *Québécois* were forced into that position by fifteen years of provocations and disappointments. And to this day, few Canadians recognize that it was a national tragedy and a betrayal of Canada's reputation for civility and compromise to have built up the hopes of an entire people only to dash them – more than

---

* As it was not in power, the Parti québécois could not take advantage of this surge and call a referendum. By early 1995, support had dropped to 45 per cent, but rose again to 49 per cent by the time of the referendum. But even that figure exaggerated the depth of support for real independence, which declined to 29 per cent if sovereignty was defined to include the loss of Canadian citizenship and passports (Dubuc, *À mes amis souverainistes*, pp. 30–1, 49).

† Jean Chrétien was Canada's Liberal prime minister and Jean Charest headed the country's Progressive Conservative party. Both had campaigned prominently against Quebec independence.

once – at the final hour. One of the enduring consequences is the absence of any interest in re-opening constitutional discussions, even to repair problems like an unelected federal Senate that have very little to do with Quebec.

Even after the referendum, Quebeckers have sometimes been offended by the denigration of their elected leaders by other Canadians. In December 2000, the *indépendantiste* premier Lucien Bouchard was invited to attend the inauguration of a new Mexican president as a "national" leader but his invitation was downgraded, reportedly at the request of the Canadian government; Bouchard decided not to attend.[65] And in April 2001, Bouchard's successor Bernard Landry was denied the right to address a word of welcome to the heads of state congregating in Quebec City for the "Summit of the Americas."[66] In both cases, the federal government was trying to limit the possibility of political mischief by men dedicated to breaking up the country. But, to many people in Quebec, this lack of courtesy was much worse than any damage it was intended to prevent.

Since 1995, many Quebeckers have turned in upon themselves, nursed their wounds, or tried to become an independent nation in their own minds. But many others have maintained or recovered their sense of balance, and it is French speakers – not English ones – who are spearheading a more confident and outward-looking society. Language – and the laws and structures introduced to promote and protect the use of French – are less of a flashpoint than they used to be. But deep grudges and worries persist and the issue can surge out of nowhere to centre stage.

In late 2014, nearly 177 years after French Canadian rebels were defeated there, the presence of four English words on their monument at Saint-Denis-sur-Richelieu raised tempers again. When the monument was erected in 1913, it carried the message "Honour to the Patriots" in both languages, but, at the request of two prominent nationalist organizations, the English phrase was covered with a brass plaque in 1987. That plaque had disappeared, presumably stolen because of high copper prices. Nationalists insisted that it be replaced before that year's commemoration, as they were insulted to see English on the monument. The town's mayor appealed for calm, doubting it would make sense to spend money on something that would almost certainly be stolen again.[67] On the other side of the language divide, seventy residents of Montreal's English-speaking Côte-St-Luc community signed a petition in August 2017, asking Loto-Québec to deny the Société Saint-Jean-Baptiste (a prominent nationalist organization) the right to run a kiosk at a local shopping centre. "Separatists are not welcome here," wrote one of the signatories. Surprisingly, even in a slow-news month, the *Montreal Gazette* devoted half a page to this small controversy.[68]

"Bonjour/Hi"

The politics of language are still so convoluted that, at a "town-hall" meeting in Quebec's Eastern Townships in January 2017, the prime minister of Canada – whose father introduced official bilingualism in the 1970s – chose to answer English questions in French. He explained later that he was merely trying to respect the pre-eminence of that language in Quebec. Critics accused him of "currying favour" with Quebec nationalists and scoring "cheap political points." Another suggested that even staunch defenders of the French language, like René Lévesque, would have been more courteous.[69] Quebec's premier and the leader of the Opposition (head of the major independence party) both said that they would have answered in English. Yet in November 2017, both men supported a unanimous motion in the National Assembly discouraging store owners from greeting customers with the all-inclusive "Bonjour/Hi."[70]

Until the late 1960s, the Quebec government was in fact quite relaxed about the status of French. The first language law stressed the importance of French but guaranteed freedom of choice at school. But a sinking birth rate among French speakers, the gravitation of immigrants towards English, and a desire to promote professional opportunities for *Québécois*, especially in Montreal, spurred further action. A 1972 public inquiry found that French-speaking managers were obliged to work largely in

English and that the *Québécois* ranked twelfth among fourteen ethnic groups in average earnings. In response, Robert Bourassa's Liberal government introduced the controversial Bill 22, the Official Language Act, declaring French the official language of Quebec's public sector, steering immigrant children unable to pass an English test into French schools, and encouraging the use of French in the corporate sector.[71] In 1977, the first Parti québécois government tightened the screws further, forcing all children to attend French schools (unless their parents had studied in English), requiring all public signage to be in French, and establishing an agency – the Office québécois de la langue française (Quebec Office of the French Language, OQLF) – to police implementation.

In one respect, these laws were the application of pure common sense, but they were also among the most illiberal actions of a Western government in modern times. Not only were they a gross violation of the rights of parents to choose how their children would be educated; they also created demons on both sides of the language issue. Camille Laurin, who was culture minister from 1976 to 1984, instilled terror across large sections of the English-speaking population, especially among older people who had spent their entire lives in Quebec and doubted their ability to master another language late in life. The laws led to the departure of tens of thousands of Quebeckers – the largest displacement of people in Canadian history since the British expulsion of the Acadians in 1755 and the federal government's resettlement of Japanese Canadians in the interior of British Columbia during the Second World War. True, those upheavals were compulsory rather than voluntary; but some of the architects of the language laws undoubtedly hoped for such departures. Many Quebeckers – including some of the most talented – left reluctantly and, even now, three-quarters of Quebec's English-speaking PhDs leave each year.[72] Some are simply following attractive job opportunities; others may be uncomfortable working in French; but many also feel unwelcome or unvalued and resent the revanchist mean-spiritedness that still infects an influential minority of *Québécois*.

Obnoxious and abusive as the language laws seemed to English speakers, the new rules proved highly successful in establishing French as the working language of Quebec. Indeed, there has been so much progress on that front that purists often underestimate it. Bilingual Quebeckers will astound visitors by their ability to switch from one language to the other without betraying which is their mother tongue. Most Quebeckers now work principally in French, and even those who do not can generally be counted upon to be considerate. In fact, many highly tortured conversations occur in French between English speakers meeting for the first time who presume that the other speaks French and, even once they suspect the truth, do not switch back to English for fear of insulting the other person's French.

One of the surprising facts about Quebec is not how many English still speak no French (about 30 per cent) but rather how many *Québécois* still speak no English (60 per cent).[73] This is a good sign for nationalists, but a sad one for those who worry about Quebec's long-term economic prospects and conceive of a society that is proud of its culture and cosmopolitan at the same time.

Perhaps understandably, the head of the OQLF was reluctant to see me, given the long history of controversy surrounding its operations. (Perhaps the most famous was the "Pastagate" fuss of 2013 caused by overly zealous language inspectors questioning the use of Italian words on an Italian restaurant menu. The OQLF head resigned shortly afterwards.) The OQLF has tried hard to adapt its approach. For example, it no longer cites legal chapter-and-verse in its initial correspondence with companies accused of infringing Quebec's language laws. About 99 per cent of the two to three thousand complaints they receive from the public each year (mostly about product labelling or English-only instruction manuals) are settled amicably.

While the OQLF would be the last place to expect complacency on the subject, it believes that the status of the French language has been stabilized for now, with about 80 per cent of Quebeckers using it at work.[74] The greatest contributing factor was the shift dictated by the 1977 language law, with 89 per cent of immigrant children now attending French schools, compared with only 15 per cent in 1975. The emphasis is now on positive reinforcement rather than policing, through the awarding of prizes to exemplary companies and individuals and the use of more flexible methods of language instruction (such as deploying university students to teach French to Chinese convenience store owners on their premises).

The OQLF's website is an international resource for linguists and writers and, according to the Paris newspaper *Le Monde*, the premier tool for editors seeking French versions of modern technical terms. The OQLF also receives regular visits from other minority peoples like the Catalans, the Welsh, and the Flemish. Surprisingly, it now interprets its mission more broadly than just protecting the national language. "Just as the reinstatement of French allowed the *Québécois* to catch up economically," Robert Vézina, head of the OQLF, told me, "we believe that all Quebeckers should now see the French language as a means of ensuring that immigrants have fair access to jobs and public services and develop a sense of belonging."[75] Seeing language as an instrument of social cohesion and even social justice is a refreshing change from the years when the OQLF was regarded by some as setting groups of citizens against each other.

"Noisy Evolution"

Progress in protecting the French language, however, has not satisfied everyone, and deep anxiety remains about Quebec's identity, especially among older people. Some observers have overlooked just how long that identity has been adapting. After the Second World War, as professors, artists, and poets debated Quebec's future, the society around them was being transformed almost beyond recognition. For more than two hundred years, being "French Canadian" meant not just a pride in preserving one's language and culture but also a deep attachment to the Catholic faith, the soil, and the rural virtues that went with them. As a result, Quebec was the last province in Canada to grant women the vote (in 1940), twenty-three years after Ontario and twenty years after the United States.[76]

Quebec's geographical isolation made it a custodian of "old school" French values well beyond the time when some of them (like a highly regimented, Vatican-oriented Catholicism) had weakened in France itself. Under Nazi occupation, France could no longer nurture French culture overseas, and Quebec became an important centre for publication and French-language studies. A young Haitian, Pierre Salgado, who was forced by the Occupation to study medicine at the University of Montreal, found a version of France in North America that had "stayed pure, faithful to its eternal traditions, loyal to its language, culture, and civilizing mission."[77] Another sign of the "old France" was that Quebec's elites sided mainly with Marshal Pétain (head of France's puppet government at Vichy) rather than the leader of the "Free French," Charles de Gaulle.

The pillars of that Quebec began tumbling well before the Quiet Revolution. In fact, most historians now question whether the 22 June 1960 election, which brought a new technocratic elite to power, was really the major watershed everyone assumed at the time. Some now regard it as merely a "noisy evolution." By the early 1950s, most French Canadians were already living in Montreal, Quebec City, or their suburbs, and even in the countryside, more than half the population was no longer on the farm but working in mining or pulp and paper and other resource-based industries. During the 1950s, high-school attendance doubled and enrolments in higher education rose by 50 per cent, as French speakers recognized that they were trapped in low-level jobs and had been misled into believing – often by the church – that academic studies were suitable only for those who wanted to be priests, doctors, or lawyers.

There was even tension between church and state. When Montreal's Archbishop Joseph Charbonneau sided with striking asbestos workers by raising funds for their families after Sunday masses in 1949, Premier Maurice Duplessis arranged for him to be re-assigned to Victoria, BC, where he ended his life as a chaplain at an old people's home.[78] Moreover, what was termed

La Grande Noirceur (the "Great Blackness") of the pre-1960 years had already been pierced by the bright lights of modern culture. In the 1940s and 1950s, there were more jazz clubs per capita in Montreal – the hometown of Oscar Peterson, Oliver Jones, and Louis Hopper – than in New York. There, too, Jackie Robinson broke the professional baseball colour barrier by playing with the Montreal Royals and becoming almost as popular as the hockey star Maurice Richard.[79] Contacts with Europe during the Second World War and the arrival of television in the 1950s were also fundamental in opening Quebec to the outside world.

During the same period, Quebec intellectuals and artists were testing their wings on an international stage. Sometimes that exploration was painful. André Laurendeau, who became chief editorial writer for the nationalist Montreal paper *Le Devoir* (1958–68) and co-chair of the Royal Commission on Bilingualism and Biculturalism (1963–8), said that it took him five years to recover from the wounds inflicted upon him by his "mother" culture while he was studying in Paris. Others weathered French pretension and paternalism towards their "rural" cousins more successfully. Quebec's unofficial poet laureate Félix Leclerc not only started his career as a songwriter in France in the 1950s but also inspired others, like Jacques Brel and Georges Brassens, to follow his lead as a singer-poet. Leclerc was so attached to French culture that he stole an iron letter from the gravestone of the seventeenth-century poet La Fontaine at Père Lachaise cemetery. ("It had almost fallen off, held barely in place by a 300-year-old screw, so I tore it off respectfully and stuffed it in my pocket. It's now on my wall in my attic in Canada on the shores of the Lake of Two Mountains and I am taking good care of it.")[80] Leclerc thrived as a bridge between Quebec and France, comfortable with his double origins and feeling no need to suppress one or the other.[81]

The 1960 election accelerated the modernization of Quebec's economy and introduced a safety net to help parts of the population adapt. The new Liberal government sowed the seeds not only of a new nationalism but also – fifty years later – of a surge of self-confidence among younger people who took the *Québécois* reappropriation of the economy for granted and no longer felt anxious about their identity.[82] According to Daniel Salée, professor of political science at Concordia University in Montreal, the achievements of the Quiet Revolution had "perverse" effects on the national consciousness of those now under forty-five who had never had to swallow the humiliation of signing labour contracts in English or answering to English bosses or regarding the phrase "French Canadian businesses" as a contradiction in terms.

Another major development that the young now take for granted was the 1992 North American Free Trade Agreement (NAFTA), which the Quebec's *indépendantiste* government championed alongside a Conservative federal prime minister (Brian Mulroney) against the reservations of left-leaning English Canadians. NAFTA was seen as a means of broadening Quebec's markets and demonstrating its ability to stand on its own two feet. But its success, too, had unforeseen effects for nationalists by weakening the argument that Quebec needed to separate for economic reasons.[83]

A few years before he was asked to co-chair a public enquiry on "reasonable accommodations" for newcomers, Charles Taylor observed that people with strong views on the subject often regard identity as something relatively finite, while young people and those who have travelled widely have trouble imagining what it means to be a "true" *Québécois*. They are conscious of having a range of interests, loyalties, and values, all of which keep evolving, and they are uncomfortable with the idea of freezing the boundaries of that exploration.[84]

This cauldron of conflicting outlooks has been heated further by mass immigration over the last thirty years.

2

Diversity

In 1982, a number of Haitian taxi drivers in Montreal were fired because some white clients refused to ride with them. Dorval Airport even changed its regulations to make it harder for them to work there. As a result, the Quebec Human Rights Commission (QHRC) held its first-ever public hearings.[1] Thirty-five years later, many Quebeckers will find this hard to believe, not because racism has been magically exorcised from their society but rather because Quebec has become so diverse after decades of mass immigration that differences of one kind or another – especially in the metropolis – have almost become the norm. A third of Montreal's taxi drivers are now Haitian, and the city has the highest proportion of immigrants in that job (84 per cent) in all of Canada.[2] Quebec has always had English-speaking sovereignists and French-speaking monarchists, but now it also has a substantial number of African lumberjacks.

The society has become so "colour-blind" that the organizers of Montreal's Saint Jean-Baptiste parade on 24 June 2017 (Quebec's "national" day) were completely flummoxed by a video on social media showing black teenagers pushing a float with only white people on it. The organizers had gone out of their way to involve different cultural communities in the event and said it was a mere accident that three volunteers from one high school should have attracted such attention.[3] Sometimes, such self-assurance can curdle into insensitivity. A spectacular example was the July 2018 cancellation of the world-renowned director Robert Lepage's show *Slav* by the Montreal International Jazz Festival. Dedicated to the history of black slave music, it became embroiled in the US debate about "cultural appropriation," as very few of the performers were black. Two weeks later, Lepage was in trouble again for the play *Kanata* depicting the historic subjugation of Canada's First Peoples. Of the thirty-four actors in the production, none was Indigenous. Defenders of Lepage ("You don't need to be Danish to play Hamlet") made no headway against those suggesting that Lepage should have been more thoughtful and aware of the risks he was running.[4] No one accused him of racism.

Openness to Diversity

In fact, in a society that many nationalists regard as under siege, a remarkable number of people profess themselves open to diversity. A 2015 QHRC survey showed that 92 per cent of Quebeckers had positive attitudes to the handicapped. They also respected people of colour (88 per cent), homosexuals (84 per cent), citizens of other ethnic origins (76 per cent), and followers of other religions (68 per cent). However, they were less open to customizing school menus for religious reasons (43 per cent) or allowing prayer spaces in colleges and universities (38 per cent). Nor were faiths treated equally. Very few Quebeckers (5 per cent) cared about a person wearing a cross, but 25 per cent objected to a kippah, 30 per cent to a turban, and 49 per cent to a veil.

When the survey results were published, QHRC's head Jacques Frémont emphasized how much public attitudes had evolved: "Imagine how low the results for the LGBTQ community or recent immigrants would have been in 1975." "But," he added, "there are still some blind spots."[5] For example, while a third of Montrealers are from a visible minority (Africans, Arabs, Hispanics, South Asians, Filipinos, Chinese, Vietnamese, etc.), only 7 per cent of the city's police officers were drawn from their ranks in 2014. The provincial police force was even less representative, with only 26 such employees in a total of 5,700.[6] Economically, too, visible minorities lag far behind the rest of society. Recent immigrants are generally poorer than native Quebeckers, but Africans and Asians are five times more likely to have low incomes than those arriving from the United States.[7] Attitudes to Quebec's First Peoples are also, to say the least, conflicted, ranging from utter indifference to a mild sense of guilt at their inferior economic and social conditions.

Quebec's comfort with diversity carries a special poignancy. For a long time, the *Québécois* themselves felt like a minority in their own society, either in fact (as Montreal had an English-speaking majority until about 1850) or in the way they were treated by the dominant class. In the early 1970s, when a friend of mine moved to Westmount (Montreal's most affluent Anglo-Saxon neighbourhood) his neighbours greeted him with the words, "We only speak French to our maid." Then, they asked him where he had lived before. "On Saint Joseph Boulevard," he replied (a prominent artery in the French-speaking heart of the city). "Where's that?" they reacted. That wasn't the only rebuff he suffered. His colleagues at the French-language college where he taught refused to visit him at his new address as he had now "sold out to the English."

Once the *Québécois* became *maîtres chez nous* (masters in our own house), which was the rallying cry of the Quiet Revolution, some of these former victims of discrimination turned against the English-speaking population with a venom that the "new" minority found hard to understand. I remember the terror with which my parents watched television during the debate about the 1977 language law and the 1980 and 1995 referendums. Their very right to be Quebeckers – not just to speak English – appeared to hang in the balance. Apart from street riots in the largely Italian Montreal suburb of Saint Léonard in 1969 over the government's intention to deny immigrants the right to send their children to English schools, change occurred largely through the ballot box. But the tension and resentment on both sides remained high for a very long time. Two of the ministers who spearheaded the introduction of the language laws were psychiatrists. Thirty years later, a Quebec senator in Ottawa told me: "People do not delegate their sovereignty to elected officials so as to have them play with their brains and change their mentalities. A politician's job is to fix concrete problems, a road here, a school there."[8]

Nationalist demonizing of English speakers led to a natural counterattack, which was sharp at first but diminished over time. For decades, English Quebeckers in Montreal's West Island peered through newspapers with magnifying glasses, like clerks in Dickensian counting houses, trying to pinpoint practices apparently targeting them: relating horror stories about the Office of the French Language; writing letters to the *Gazette* to complain of various slights by French speakers; and insisting that unilingual-French traffic signs were a danger to public safety, especially to cousins visiting from the United States. Often, the letter writers seemed petty; but sometimes they had a point. Those who prided themselves on trying to speak French could be made to feel inadequate because of their accent or limited vocabulary. Even those who spoke French *too well* because they had lived or worked abroad were sometimes objects of suspicion, as if they had made a conscious effort to outgrow a Quebec accent.

The Challenge of Immigration

These English-French tensions have now been overtaken by a deeper, more complicated worry. Still the world's second-largest French-speaking city, Montreal is also one of the most cosmopolitan places in North America. Almost 40 per cent of the city's population were born in another country or to parents who immigrated to Canada. While the number is much higher in Toronto (76 per cent) and Vancouver (68 per cent), the challenge of absorbing such a large number of newcomers in a society that is culturally insecure is particularly acute.[9] As in Canada more generally, the smoothness with which immigrants have adapted may be a function of their very numbers. As the American writer E.B.

White wrote about an even more diverse place in 1949, "The citizens of New York are tolerant not only from disposition but from necessity. The city has to be tolerant, otherwise it would explode in a radioactive cloud of hate and rancor and bigotry. If the people were to depart even briefly from the peace of cosmopolitan intercourse, the town would blow up higher than a kite."[10]

But one feature of mass immigration has caused special anxiety. In January 2007, the village of Hérouxville (which did not have a single immigrant) sparked international headlines by introducing a code of conduct for new residents that, among other things, prohibited covering one's face and stoning, mutilating, or burning women. Many Quebeckers were amused rather than offended by this, as it reflected a mounting sense of frustration about Islamist extremism around the world and, closer to home, the special demands of some religious minorities. Hassidic Jews in Montreal had insisted that a YMCA surround their exercise rooms with frosted glass to prevent their young men from seeing women in gym outfits, while Muslims had petitioned for halal offerings at school cafeterias. Within a month, with an election approaching, the government appointed a public commission to look into the question of "reasonable accommodations" for minority groups. (See "Bouchard-Taylor Commission" below.)

Five years later, the issue was still a live wire. In 2013, a minority *indépendantiste* government proposed a "Charter of Quebec Values" that would bar government employees from wearing Muslim headscarves. The measure was intended to ease the fears of some of its supporters but also apparently to attract rural votes in the next election, but the debate that followed turned ugly. Muslim families picnicking on Mount Royal were occasionally shouted at by passers-by, while young Muslim women in the Metro were insulted by strangers. Even staff in the office of the minister responsible for the Charter sobbed at the damage that was being done.[11] To the annoyance of some and relief of many, the government and its dreaded Charter were defeated at the next election. But suspicion of Muslims persisted across Quebec. In March 2015, a national poll found that 82 per cent of Canadians wanted the niqab (the full veil) banned at citizenship ceremonies, and that opposition was highest in Quebec (93 per cent).[12] And on 29 January 2017 – almost exactly ten years after the Hérouxville code of conduct made headlines – a young man walked into a mosque in a suburb of Quebec City and shot six people dead as they prayed.

This discomfort with Islam is part of a broader pattern in Western countries that have admitted a large number of Muslim immigrants. But in Quebec it is associated with two concepts that have a particular resonance there: *laïcité* (secularism) and multiculturalism.

Laïcité

French commitment to the separation of church and state has its roots in the Age of Enlightenment (1685–1789) with its sometimes sarcastic, sometimes restrained, criticism of the role of religion in everyday life. Voltaire's *Treatise on Tolerance* (1763) oozes reasonableness and remains as relevant today as when it was published, but his play *Mahomet* (Mohammed) was so biting it would have made the 2005 Danish cartoons of the Prophet seem innocuous. (The French authorities allowed the play to be performed for four nights but shut it down when they realized that it was an attack not just on Islam but also on religion more generally.) The crispest summary of the ideal of secularism in the "public space" was that of Condorcet, author of *The Idea of Progress* (1794): "One day, the sun will shine only on free men, who will be ruled only by their own Reason, and there will no longer be tyrants and slaves, or priests and their idiots, except in history books or on the stage."[13] When the working people of Paris took over the city in March–May 1871, in one of the proudest – and bloodiest – chapters of anarchist history, they outlawed the teaching of religion in school out of respect for "the consciences of young people." It is in the classroom, one poster in the fourth *arrondissement* declared, that "all religious concepts should be subject to examination by Reason and Science."[14]

Thereafter, modern-day *laïcité* in France was not the product of a sensible debate about the role of religion in society. Instead, it was the culmination of three decades of impassioned anti-clericalism that reached its peak in 1905 when the French government confiscated all church properties and closed down most of the country's religious communities. More than a century later, this putting of religion "in its place" is not only widely accepted but also deeply rooted in French culture. Almost no one objects to having two wedding ceremonies (the civil one being the legally valid one), and French bishops are happy that the state is responsible for maintaining the country's ancient cathedrals. The only exception to the rule – the carry-over of German practices in Alsace-Lorraine, where priests are paid state salaries and bishops ride around in official limousines – stands in stark contrast to the general policy. In small towns across France, regardless of their political affiliations, mayors have to provide for the maintenance of the local church and presbytery. Priests in turn have tried to keep a low profile and, until recently, avoided wearing cassocks in the street.

Similarly, for as long as anyone can remember, French government employees have been forbidden to wear prominent religious symbols. In 2004, exasperated by the increasing use of the Muslim headscarf, the French banned it in state schools and have recently considered extending the policy to university campuses. Even parents picking up their children at the end of the day are discouraged from wearing them. In 2011, France went further and forbade the wearing of the burqa (the full body veil) in public, subject to a fine of 150 euros and a course in citizenship. Anyone forcing a woman to cover her face risked a 30,000-euro fine. Belgium, Denmark, several German states, and towns in Italy and Spain have followed suit. Austria has forbidden all children under ten from wearing it, while countries like Switzerland and the Netherlands are considering action.[15]

Even the European Court of Human Rights, perhaps the greatest bastion of individual liberties on Earth, has justified these bans on the grounds than communal harmony overrides a person's right to religious expression.[16] The one exception is the United Kingdom, where the right-wing UKIP Party called for a ban in January 2010 but the education minister said that it was "not British" to tell people what to wear on the street.[17] In August 2018, Prime Minister Theresa May chastised her former foreign secretary Boris Johnson for saying that women wearing burqas looked like "letter boxes" or "bank robbers"; yet, even he was not calling for them to be banned.[18] In contrast, in France, even personal behaviour can prove compromising. In April 2018, the country's highest administrative court denied citizenship to an Algerian woman for refusing to shake hands with male officials at her naturalization ceremony. Her action, the court ruled, "in a place and at a moment that are symbolic, reveals a lack of assimilation."[19]

In Quebec, the marriage of French and British values and the restraining influence of Canada's Supreme Court have prevented it from following in France's footsteps. As a result, until recently there was no prohibition of the headscarf of any kind, because many Quebeckers did not recognize the problem that banning it was meant to solve. Yet, tempers have flared around the issue. At the height of the debate about the Charter, a government minister said that public employees who insisted on wearing religious symbols would have to give up their jobs. "It will be their choice, if they place religion above everything else, above the public interest, above the law." The same week, the mayor of Montreal complained that the government had invented a crisis out of thin air as the city had not received a single complaint about religious symbols.[20]

In October 2017, after dragging its feet for three years, the Liberal government bowed to public pressure and insisted that people's faces should not be covered when delivering or receiving public services. This fell far short of what most other political parties wanted and affected perhaps one hundred people in a society of eight million who routinely wear the full veil. Other politicians wanted to ban every kind of headscarf in the public service and at the very least among people in positions of authority (judges, police officers, prison guards). It was unclear whether the government's small concession would fend off the appetite for more extreme measures or end up being a finger in the dike. In the days that followed, a slightly embarrassed government made clear that no one would be asked to get off a bus or be denied emergency health care because of what she was wearing. Nor was it certain that the law would survive a challenge in the Supreme Court. In October 2018, the new Quebec government announced that it would ban the wearing of headscarves by those in positions of public authority and extended that definition to include teachers. In response to a public outcry, it backtracked almost immediately and said that the rule would only apply to new hires. Not surprisingly, these measures caused discomfort elsewhere in Canada, which saw it as an expression of Islamophobia.

Revolt against Catholicism

The situation is more complicated than that. Ironically, nervousness about headscarves has been most intense in rural Quebec, where few people have ever seen a hijab, niqab, or burqa. But, in the cities, many "progressives" rallied to the cause for reasons that had less to do with Islam than with the Catholic Church. For centuries, religious faith had been central to Quebec's identity but, by the second half of the twentieth century, many people saw the church as a reactionary force opposing modernization and keeping French Canadians in a near-infantile state. Not surprisingly, given the general nature of upheavals in public attitudes, the baby was thrown out with the bath water. Little credit was given to the institution for its attempts to reform itself or for its positive role in preserving Quebec's culture and educating generation after generation, including the one that ushered in the Quiet Revolution. But the church had certainly invited opprobrium for its outsized role in politics and a rigid form of ritual and submission that France had shaken off fifty years before.

In 1960, for the first time, Quebeckers insisted on a major government role in health and education. Until then, 40 per cent of Catholic clergy served in the public service as teachers, doctors, nurses, and social workers, with clerics even holding key positions in government ministries.[21] More than anything else, the creation of a ministry of education signalled that public policy rather than the Catholic Church would now drive the training of the young. But this did not happen until 1964 and, even then, at the very top of a highly reformist government, there was resistance to making education completely non-confessional. In May 1961, while handing out diplomas at the University of Montreal, Premier Jean Lesage said that he would never accept the creation of "atheist schools" or "help propagate godlessness," which was "a mental illness."[22]

Quebec's revolt against Catholicism was also related to the pill. By the 1950s, like their counterparts elsewhere in the West, women in the province were growing keenly interested in controlling their reproductive lives. The church, which had opposed all forms of artificial birth control since 1930, now agreed to review its teaching. In 1963, Pope John XXIII appointed a commission of bishops and theologians to study the issue, and his successor, Paul VI, expanded it to include women and lay people. In 1965, it recommended relaxing church rules on the subject, and Western bishops (including those in Quebec) began turning a blind eye to official teaching. When, three years later, the Pope announced that he was overruling the commission and holding the line, the revulsion in rich countries was audible. Bishops in Belgium, the Netherlands, Switzerland, Scandinavia, and the United States dissented publicly from the decision, and the "faithful" took note of the controversy.[23] Like most Catholics in North America, Quebec women now ignored church teaching on contraception completely. Others went further, turning their backs on the church altogether, tired of the institution's overbearing attitudes and appalled not only by the intrusion of celibate men into their private lives but even more by their implied lack of respect for gender equality. Like a wound-up elastic, Quebec women snapped back smartly. Within a generation Quebec went from having the highest birth rate in Canada to having the lowest.

It is a deep commitment to improving the rights of women and a suspicion of religion in general that have given anti-Muslim feelings in Quebec their particular edge. In 2013, 81 per cent of Quebeckers thought that gender equality should prevail over freedom of religion.[24] Listen to one *Québécoise* writing to an Algerian friend in 2014:

> Quebec was under the heel of the Catholic Church for 400 years. It's scarcely an exaggeration to say that they were for us what the Taliban is for you. It took us all that time to rid ourselves of its ridiculous dogmas and beliefs. Do you think we're going to let another religion enter our lives and our public space? Do you really believe I'm happy that my granddaughter's teacher wears a headscarf that seems to say "See? I'm better than you, because I practice my religion"? We are now a people freed of religion. So I ask you to join our other immigrants, the Italians, the Chinese, the Greeks, the Vietnamese, the Latin Americans, who practice their religions, but more discreetly. Why is it easy for them and not for you?[25]

Religious Symbols

Believers in *laïcité* embrace a broad range of opinion. Some see it, positively, as "a desire to live together by rising above our differences and stressing our common humanity rather than living behind cultural and religious walls."[26] Others regard it as a licence for attacking all forms of religious belief and promoting secularism for its own sake rather than just as a safe ground for pluralist expression. The 2014 debate over the proposed Charter opened a chasm as wide as the one caused by the 1977 language law. The small *indépendantiste* party Québec solidaire, which opposed the Charter as antithetical to its own belief in an inclusive society, faced a backlash and had to defend its position even to its own members. "Let's not get carried away," its leaders said. "We are not saying that all defenders of *laïcité* are racist, xenophobe, or anti-Muslim. But let's also recognize that some xenophobes use *laïcité* to make a virtue of discriminating against people. They use the word as a veneer to mask their fear of people who are different from them."[27] Others saw the matter as a mere question of courtesy. Arguing that no religion absolutely requires the wearing of symbols, one commentator drew a parallel with bad weather in Quebec: "If someone refuses to take off his boots when he comes into my house, particularly when it is slushy outside, he is being impolite. Even if the host says 'No, no, it doesn't matter,' the guest should still be considerate."[28]

In September 2013, an Afghan who had been living in Montreal for twenty-five years wrote to the Montreal newspaper *La Presse* to express his admiration of Quebec's social services, civil peace, legal system, religious liberty, and freedom of expression: "In exchange for all this, surely the least I can do is to fit in. What's so difficult about removing a religious symbol at work in exchange for all that our society is doing for us?"[29] One answer might be that no one should feel obliged to surrender any of the liberties the Afghan was happy about without a strong social reason for doing so.

Unfortunately, the debate in Quebec centred on Muslim rather than Christian, Jewish, or Sikh symbols. "What's so special about the headscarf?" its defenders ask. Many Quebeckers (including a large number of Muslims) certainly regard it as a sign of female submission, religious exhibitionism, and the promotion of Islamic values. But to those who wear it, the veil can express a respect for tradition, personal modesty, a sense of fashion, and even pure convenience. Undoubtedly, some women don it against their wills, but who will determine that? And, in the view of those who believe in inclusiveness, if only one woman in Quebec wore a headscarf willingly, surely a liberal society should want to defend her right to do so.

Bouchard-Taylor Commission

A redeeming feature of the debate is that it has been open and unrestrained. In early 2007, pressed into a corner by a number of local controversies, the Quebec government asked two of the province's most respected intellectuals, the philosopher Charles Taylor and sociologist Gérard Bouchard, to look into the issue of whether society should make "reasonable accommodations" for the needs of religious minorities. Their public hearings acted as a lightning rod for extreme views, especially in the rural areas. Journalists were often shocked by the pure racism lacing many of the participants' complaints, but one columnist calculated that less than five per cent of the public's comments were truly objectionable. Elsewhere, and especially in Montreal, the range of opinions was closer to what educated Quebeckers recognized in themselves: vague, multifaceted, and sometimes self-contradictory on the same day.

The commission drew on voices that needed to be heard. An eleven-year-old boy named Jérémie Meloche-Fréchette (accompanied by his grandmother, who undoubtedly helped prepare his submission) told the commission: "Immigrants have trouble adapting to our way of life because French is a difficult language. When they learn it, they'll understand us better. But, in the meantime, they have trouble finding work and we need to help them." Hermann Cebert, a conservative economist from Haiti, said it was wrong to believe that immigrants were part of Quebec's national dream. They came to build their "own dream," not a country, and he called for an end to social welfare for everyone, not just immigrants.[30] Sikhs insisted they did not want to impose their own values on society, but went on to say that they opposed Christmas trees in public places, wanted all religious holidays to be recognized (as in India), and refused to wear hard hats on construction sites or bicycle helmets on the street, as their turbans got in the way.[31] One journalist suggested that "if Paris was worth a Mass" (a reference to Henry IV converting to Catholicism in 1598 to sit on the French throne), "Montreal was certainly worth a few frosted windows."[32] Far from being ashamed of this outpouring of views or the supposed tarring of Quebec's image abroad, thoughtful Quebeckers welcomed the decision to debate a sometimes ugly issue in the full light of day.

In February 2008, I attended the Bouchard-Taylor Commission's final hearing in Montreal. I sat next to a Jewish Moroccan woman active in outreach to the city's "cultural communities" (i.e., minorities). At one point, she leaned over to hear what two women to my right were saying, then whispered to me with almost scientific excitement, "I am always fascinated by old-stock Quebeckers." A young woman in a headscarf got up to say that immigrants should be regarded as an enrichment rather than a threat. Other Muslims were less emollient. "Why boast about Quebec culture?" one asked. "Look at it from our point of view. The first thing we see, getting off a plane at Dorval, is a billboard telling us to prove we're men by guzzling a case of beer." An Italian Quebecker observed that Roman Catholics now needed as much protection as Muslims. Someone he knew had been asked by a colleague at work whether she was lesbian, because she was not wearing a wedding ring. "I *am*," she replied, but I don't live with anyone because I'm a practising Catholic." "*A practising Catholic?!*" her questioner exclaimed, apparently more shocked by her religious beliefs than by her sexual identity.

Multiculturalism

If the debate on religion has been intense in Quebec, scepticism about multiculturalism has been even more remarkable. Now almost synonymous with Canada itself, the policy originated in a speech that Prime Minister Pierre Elliott Trudeau gave in Parliament in 1971. Other countries, like Australia, the Netherlands, and the United Kingdom, embraced the idea and, for a while, cultural co-existence looked like becoming a standard feature of Western democracy, outside the United States. In recent years, however, under the pressure of mass immigration, it has sparked controversy and retreats, with German chancellor Angela Merkel suggesting in 2010 that "multiculturalism has utterly failed." Instead, she thought, immigrants should try harder to integrate into German society.[33] In 2015, Merkel went further and called the idea of different ethnic groups "living happily side by side" a "sham."[34] Support for it in English Canada, however, has never wavered. In a 2008 poll, multiculturalism trailed only the flag, the armed forces, and hockey as an object of national pride, outranking even Canada's trademark national health system.[35] Of course, that support is not unanimous, with other polls suggesting that a third of Canadians regard multiculturalism as a threat to social unity. A quarter of them – and half of all *indépendantistes* – see it as a danger to the future of the French language.[36]

Why is the Canadian equivalent of motherhood and apple pie controversial in Quebec? The short answer is cultural insecurity. Take one extreme view from a young writer who detects a pernicious "love triangle" between the left, Islam, and respect for cultural diversity: "According to the logic of multiculturalism, all cultures have the same value. Animist oral traditions are worth as much as the greatest masterpieces of French literature, and Beethoven's symphonies may be compared to the drum rhythms of primitive tribes."[37] (Few English Canadians would recognize this extreme statement as an aspect of multiculturalism.) Other *Québécois* are simply echoing opinions in France about the danger of creating cultural ghettoes. Many *indépendantistes* prefer the idea of *inter*-culturalism. In the words of the former Quebec premier Bernard Landry, "Think about a convergence of cultures, enriching each other's lives, *but in the French language*. This is easy because many of our new Quebeckers are from North Africa, Haiti, and Spanish- and Portuguese- speaking countries and share the Latin roots of our tongue. Multiculturalism implies independent pockets of culture, some of which will insist on special protections and even public funding, emphasizing differences rather than what we have in common. Napoleon ended official anti-Semitism in Europe but told France's Jews: 'As Jews, you have absolutely no rights. But as French citizens, you have all of them.'"[38]

However, social realities are different on opposite sides of the Atlantic. In Western Europe, economic insecurity and sharp cutbacks in national welfare systems have sparked a backlash against newcomers, forcing some of them to want to live in a parallel society.[39] In Canada, there has been little sign of this. Instead, Canadian census data suggest that immigrants integrate faster into the national community if they have a strong attachment to their own ancestry and customs.[40] Like stepping stones across a rushing river, pride in one's original culture can ease the passage into a wider set of attachments.

Nor has Canada seen the kind of ethnic disturbances that rocked the United Kingdom in 2001 or France in 2005, 2007, and 2009. Public inquiries there concluded that deindustrialization, unemployment, and racial discrimination in housing and jobs – rather than any wish to live apart – triggered the violence.

Integration

If Europeans have had second thoughts about multiculturalism, how to move beyond it is not always obvious. Many observers see the challenge as progressing from "pure" multiculturalism (the respectful co-existence of different ethnic backgrounds) through to a minimum acceptance of host-country norms ("integration") to complete absorption of newcomers ("assimilation"). One British home secretary thought that a sure sign of integration would be when immigrants supported the English cricket team against their own home countries (India, Pakistan, West Indies). A more realistic successor argued that what really mattered was the speaking of English at home.[41] Other yardsticks suggest that British equal-opportunity and anti-discrimination programs have worked. In 2010, 70 per cent of British Muslims over fifty-five felt they had more in common with non-Muslims in the UK than with fellow believers abroad. In a different study, three-quarters saw themselves as nationals, compared with only half in France and a quarter in Germany. Second-generation Muslims felt even more at home.[42] South Asian Muslims, Sikhs, and Hindus now intermarry frequently among themselves and with other British nationals. At a pinch, it is whites who are less likely to mix with minorities, rather than the other way around.[43]

Canada is also doing something right, and British values have probably played a part – even in Quebec. English Canada has generally aimed at a "mosaic" or "salad bowl" rather than the American "melting pot." Live and let live, muddling through, and the vestiges of a shared Commonwealth history have helped old and new Canadians get along with a minimum of friction and formal programs. Instead of cricket loyalties or the language spoken at the dinner table, immigrants show that they feel at home in other ways. I think of the taxi driver at the height of the fuss about a Charter of Values who handed me a leaflet urging fellow Muslims to boycott Quebec lamb and buy meat for their next major feast in Ontario. A more serious sign of integration was international student assessment results in 2017 showing immigrant children in Canada performing as well as anyone else, contradicting the theory that culturally cohesive and compact societies (like Singapore) have a unique advantage.[44]

The challenge of "integration" in Quebec is of course much harder, given the special sensitivities and pitfalls. The government devotes considerable resources to French-language training and other programs of adaptation but cannot force immigrants to enrol in them. Not surprisingly, attendance has been dropping. There is also serious concern about new Quebeckers gravitating to the English-language education system after high school. The equivalent of an entire French-language junior college (cégep) is emptied every year because of these departures. And many people – not just ardent nationalists – wonder what this will mean for the shape of a future Quebec.[45]

Concern about immigration has been a constant in Quebec society and one does not need to be illiberal to share it. The internationally respected political scientist Michael Ignatieff has argued that too much immigration too fast "can overwhelm the capacity of societies to treat people fairly and help them make a new start."[46] Even the independence movement's greatest figure, René Lévesque, renowned for his humanity, was concerned about its long-term effects. "We have given ourselves a Ministry of Immigration," he said in 1970. "The one in Ottawa which has the real power has the right to continue to drown us. Ours simply keeps track of the drowning."[47]

Until the October 2018 election, when one major party recommended cutbacks, Quebeckers have been less concerned about total numbers of immigrants than about the cultural concessions that they were expected to make to newcomers. In 2005, only 18 per cent of Quebeckers thought immigration a "bad thing," compared with 62 per cent in Germany, 50 per cent in France, and 44 per cent in the United Kingdom and the United States. Among Canada's ten provinces and the United States' fifty states, Quebec was the seventh highest in welcoming immigrants per head.

But the demands of some newcomers were another matter. In a 2007 survey, at the height of the debate over "reasonable accommodation," the same proportion of immigrants as Quebeckers as a whole (70 per cent) thought the situation had got out of hand.[48] More recently, in a May 2018 poll, possibly influenced by anti-immigrant views in the United States and Europe, 76 per cent of Quebeckers said that newcomers "too often impose their values and religion on us."[49]

Majority Rights

That concern about immigration has grown stronger and broader in the last ten years. Not only does the survival of the French language seem in the balance; many worry that Quebec's very personality is growing fuzzier. In a perceptive essay entitled *Nous* (Us), the *indépendantiste* politician Jean-François Lisée summed up the appeal of nativism a decade before it propelled Donald Trump into the White House. "For twenty years, we have praised tolerance and cultural exchange and supported the rights of minorities. No doubt, we had to do this. Correct wrongs. Make room for others. Impose respect. But, in the process, Quebeckers have lost their sense of balance. In stretching the boundaries of identity, we, the majority, have lost a sense of ourselves, and this is all the more true because our own way of life – such as our attitude to religion – has also been evolving."[50]

According to Lisée, the challenge for Quebec, and also for France, the United Kingdom, and the United States, is to recognize that the majority now wants its own rights respected. Progressives may see this demand as ignorant and consider a complex multicultural world as the only one imaginable. Populists may use public impatience to sow division and try rolling back some minority rights. But, in Lisée's mind, most politicians should now foster a new social balance in which all can find their place.

Denying this would mean taking down the Cross on Mount Royal, or putting up an illuminated Star of David or Crescent next to it, or rotating them on an annual basis so that no one would occupy that space permanently. The Cross is there, on its own, for a reason. Not because of some hegemony or superiority, but because of the predominance of a group that has defined and will continue to define the historical, cultural, linguistic, and economic space within which all Quebeckers live. They are predominant because of their strength in numbers, their vitality, and their will to endure.[51]

Others see multiculturalism as a vessel into which they can pour their disappointment about the loss of traditional values, like religious faith, the work ethic, attachment to family, and respect for authority. In a bilious 2016 essay that ran to nearly four hundred pages, the prominent Quebec sociologist Mathieu Bock-Côté denounced multiculturalism as a "political religion": "Behind the worship of diversity, we can see the crumbling of citizenship and our capacity to act collectively. Can our freedoms survive the levelling of our institutions? We are now haunted by the fear that our social bonds – our political community and national identity – are being frayed. And, if the word were allowed in polite circles, some of us would denounce this as decadence."[52]

Fortunately, as we saw at the beginning of this chapter, Quebeckers are generally comfortable with a society that is now highly diverse. That attitude has deep roots and is sometimes attributed to the dominant role of women and feminine values in the society.[53] Others see centuries of intermarriage and contact with Quebec's First Peoples as the source of such hospitality, community, and consensus.[54]

Terry Haig grew up in New York state in the 1950s but has spent most of his life in Quebec. After forty-five years as a teacher, actor, political journalist, newspaper columnist, TV and radio personality, and sportscaster (including two years covering Montreal Expos baseball games), Terry continues to work at Radio Canada International. His respect for his adopted society is unflinching: "Let's face it, the great, great majority of Quebeckers possess an immense generosity of spirit. At least, that's been my experience. I have always felt that if a Muslim family moved next door to a Quebec family in the countryside, the next morning the *Québécois* mother would knock on the door with a home-made *pâté de poulet* [chicken pâté] as a gift."[55] In 2000, Inam Malik came from Pakistan to do a master's degree in engineering at Concordia University in Montreal. Now a technology manager with McKinsey & Co. in New York City, he looks back on his fifteen years in Quebec with utter fondness. "I was never made to feel like an outsider. No one even gave me a strange look. Elsewhere in the world, you get respect 99 percent of the time but it is all about business. I have never encountered the personal warmth that I felt in Quebec."[56]

Even opponents of multiculturalism are capable of such hospitality. They will also admit that immigrants can bring with them the very values that conservatives cherish. Concern about the role of religion and the treatment of women has complicated attitudes towards Muslims. The views and feelings of English-speaking Quebeckers are also given short shrift at times. But in every other respect Quebec's social bonds appear to be remarkably sound.

3

Solidarity

In the early 1970s, Ian Bennett and I were newly minted economists at the Department of Finance in Ottawa. I left the department in 1975, but Ian stayed on, rising steadily through the ranks, and in due course became deputy minister. As a young buck, fresh out of British Columbia, he had pithy views about Canada's French-speaking province. So, forty years later, in the safety of a private conversation with an old friend, after decades of constitutional bickering and interminable tugs of war about the "fiscal imbalance" between Ottawa and Quebec, I expected to get an earful.

Instead, Ian told me this: "Quebec has served as a social conscience for the rest of Canada. Like Saskatchewan in the 1960s on Medicare, Quebec led the way on childcare and maternity leave. Quebec has also had one of the better civil services – if not the best – in Canada, because of the high profile of public service in the French tradition and the cohesion of Quebec's corporate and government elites."

In 1991, Ian visited Quebec City to discuss the introduction of the General Services Tax (GST), Canada's value-added tax. Quebec had insisted on administering the GST itself to prevent hundreds of federal government officials from snooping into Quebec businesses, and Ian was there to finalize the details of this unique arrangement. Before leaving, he warned his opposite number that he might have trouble getting the legislation through the

National Assembly, as it was facing a firestorm in English Canada. "Not at all," his counterpart replied. "We've already talked to Parizeau (the Opposition leader) and he agrees that the new tax will be much more efficient." That cohesiveness meant that Quebec embraced change more easily than other provinces and made it more difficult for others in Canada to challenge cherished views there. "They kept us on our toes," Ian recalled. "They were tough negotiators. And they never used frivolous arguments."[1]

In April 2016, the second largest opposition party (the Coalition Avenir Québec [CAQ]) suggested that all Quebec children begin kindergarten at the age of four and that the mandatory school age be raised to eighteen, as in Ontario, New Brunswick, and eighteen US states.[2] Although it would cost eighty million dollars per year, almost immediately the Liberal government adopted the idea. At a time when elites and experts are under fire from populists, such cohesiveness may attract controversy, but there is little doubt that, in most respects, it has served Quebec well. Of course, it has also led to political conformism and blind spots, especially in the media. In 2009, the ombudsman for Radio-Canada concluded that most prominent journalists were from old Quebec families, had studied social sciences, and had been active on the left or in the independence movement. As a result, they shared the same prejudices: they were generally pro-union, anti-American, and anti-clerical. They also failed to foresee the rise of new conservative forces and the tensions caused by large-scale immigration. "Their opinions," said the ombudsman, "are so similar that our star reporters and commentators seem to compare notes on their [smart phones]."[3]

Taking Politics Seriously

That said, Quebeckers take their politics very seriously and are not easily led by the nose. Since 1867, they have created more political parties than any other province (seventy), with Ontario (sixteen) a distant runner-up.[4] While 72 per cent of UK voters participated in the June 2016 decision on membership in the European Union, 85 per cent of Quebeckers voted in the 1980 referendum on independence and 95 per cent in the second one in 1995. Quebeckers can also be decisive. Although generally conservative (60 per cent of them vote for centre-right or right-wing parties at the provincial level), in the May 2011 federal elections they swept the party that had long represented them in Ottawa (the Bloc québécois) almost completely out of office, replacing them with fifty-nine MPs from the New Democratic Party (NDP), a mildly socialist party. Until then, the NDP had had only one seat in Quebec. Some saw this wild swing as temperamental; others, as a shrewd use of the ballot box. In October 2018, Quebeckers showed again that they are not asleep at the switch, giving more than 50 per cent of their vote to two parties that did not even exist ten years before. The one that formed the government was only seven years old.

For the last fifty years, Quebec has been generally fortunate in its politicians, especially its premiers, who have been competent, down to earth, and less stark in their outlooks than some of their followers. English Quebeckers tended to think of leaders of the Parti québécois (the largest independence party) as stilted and sectarian. But even the most formal of them, Jacques Parizeau, famous for his three-piece suits and described by one disgruntled *indépendantiste* as a "cartoon of a vice-consul of the British Raj,"[5] was capable of great charm and delicacy. In France, he was invited to lunch at the home of a socialite who had set her table with little Canadian flags. A Quebec journalist, arriving early, panicked at the indiscretion, quickly scooped up the little emblems, and explained the mistake to the hostess. But, at the front door, she persisted in handing a little maple-leaf flag to her guest. "How thoughtful of you," said Parizeau, without batting an eyelash.[6]

In the 1970s, at the University of Montreal, where he taught economics, Parizeau urged an English-speaking student self-conscious about his French to practise with him every couple of weeks. That young man, David Levine, would later become a junior minister of health and one of the few prominent voices in the Jewish community supporting Quebec's independence.[7]

As a student in Montreal in the 1960s, I invited the then-minister of energy and natural resources and later first *indépendantiste* premier of Quebec, René Lévesque, to talk at our college.

I must have written to him in my own language, because I still have his gracious handwritten reply, also in English.

Some politicians, like Lévesque and Lucien Bouchard, achieved a status that was close to sainthood. Fresh from losing a leg – and almost his life – to a flesh-eating virus, Bouchard took over the leadership of the flagging pro-independence campaign in 1995 and brought it to within inches of victory. Twenty years later, the Canadian diplomat Raymond Chrétien recalled: "The moment I saw Bouchard take over, I thought that for us things would go downhill from there, that it would all become a lot more difficult. He was like the Holy Ghost, people wanted to touch him. How were we supposed to fight against that?"[8]

Pauline Marois, who was Quebec's first woman premier (2012–14) and also an *indépendantiste,* could be unconvincing in public but engaging, plucky, and self-critical in private. She recounts how, early in her career, she almost turned down a job as chief of staff to the minister of women's affairs because she had recently had her first child. Besides, she did not regard herself as a feminist. The minister – a colossus of Quebec's political scene named Lise Payette – was unfazed. "That's all right," Payette replied. "At my side, it'll be only a matter of weeks before you become one."[9] As minister of labour and income protection in the 1980s, Marois championed a welfare reform requiring young recipients to go back to school, enter apprenticeship programs, or do community work. This attempt to prevent life-long dependency on the state and allow young people to be active again in society was naturally denounced by some as a "right-wing." Some young protesters, supported by the Catholic bishops and the editorial staff of *Le Devoir,* began a hunger strike in front of the Montreal Stock Exchange. Marois told the bishops that if any of the demonstrators died it would be on their conscience rather than hers, whereupon the church persuaded them to give up. Other sensible reforms, like increasing competition among hairdressers, led to her receiving hundreds of envelopes stuffed with locks of hair. Twenty-five years later, a friend's barber still hated her.[10]

Young nationalists can also be disarming. Léo Bureau-Blouin, who co-led the 2012 "Maple Spring" student protests against higher university tuition fees, was briefly elected to the National Assembly at the age of twenty (the youngest in the history of the institution). He contributed a quarter of his parliamentary salary to community causes in his riding. ("My girl friend wasn't crazy about the idea," he admitted to me in a 2016 interview.) Later, he participated in weekly debates on an English-language Montreal radio station (CJAD) to build bridges across the linguistic communities and won a Rhodes Scholarship to pursue his legal studies at Oxford.

I asked him how he avoided a sense of defeatism in the face of apparently unstoppable demographic trends in Quebec. He thought the nationalist cause was still worth fighting for, if only to fend off the homogenizing forces of mass American culture and set an example for other small nations in the world. He hoped that Quebeckers could come together around a larger cause like fighting climate change and realize how little they could accomplish within current political boundaries. He was open to staying in a looser federation – like Switzerland – but saw little chance of constitutional reform after the scarring episodes of the 1980s and 1990s. "The tragedy of the 1995 referendum was not just that it set back the hopes of *indépendantistes* for a generation but it also undermined the case for political action in general."[11]

Of course, not everyone in Quebec politics has aspired to holiness. Some have gone to almost ludicrous lengths to test the public's patience. Lise Thibault, who was lieutenant governor (the Queen's representative in the province) for ten years and would normally have attracted sympathy because she was seventy-seven and confined to a wheelchair, pleaded guilty in December 2014 to claiming seven hundred thousand dollars in improper expenses, although she asserted that she was not a civil servant and should benefit from royal immunity. The court ruled against her and sentenced her to eighteen months in prison.[12] André Boisclair, who was briefly the leader of the Parti québécois (and the first openly gay head of any party in the province) admitted to using cocaine in his office when he was a minister but never apologized for it. During the March 2007 election, he refused to answer reporters' questions in English, claiming that he knew it only imperfectly, despite having recently completed an MA in public administration at Harvard. His party was soundly defeated, owing in no small measure to discomfort in the rural areas with his "metropolitan" ways.

Nationalists of Different Shades

Fortunately, the nationalist family is large and diverse, mixing concern for the future with varying degrees of humanity and level-headedness. For example, at the height of the controversy in 2014 over a proposed Charter of Quebec Values that would have banned the wearing of headscarves by government employees, four former leaders of the main sovereignist parties (the Parti québécois and Bloc québécois) publicly opposed the measure. One of them, the former premier Bernard Landry, told me:

> Canadians have always referred to us as a "race" and I have always said that, no, we are a *nation* but a multi-ethnic one. I am proud that we elected the first African to the National Assembly, that the Bloc sent the first Latin American *Québécois* to Ottawa, and that we had another African *Québécois* as our Minister of Culture. The first *Québécois* elected to the *Académie française* [Dany Leferrière] was born in Haiti. Four of our premiers were of Irish descent. Our culture has been enriched by others. Think just about food, which is important to the *Québécois*. The Middle Eastern *mechoui* is now very common and we owe our lamb industry to the Jewish Passover tradition. That is why I opposed the idea of a Charter of "Quebec" values. I fought all my political life to draw cultural minorities closer to the cause of Quebec independence and, in a month, the Charter destroyed thirty years of work.[13]

That sense of proportion is a perfect antidote to the demands of hardliners. Ten years ago, pressure built up to impose the use of French in all publicly funded day-care centres. Michel David of *Le Devoir*, one of Quebec's most lucid columnists (and nationalists), shook his head: "Often, a child is only a few months old when it enters a day-care centre and doesn't speak any language, let alone one or two. For the mother, it can be a painful moment, filled with guilt and worry about how the child may be treated. The least we can do is allow her a greater sense of security. So, why shouldn't she use an Italian or Spanish facility closer to home or work, if she wants to?"[14]

Unfortunately, such reasonableness is not universal and antagonizes diehards, whose bitterness can get the better of them. In late 2015, Christian Saint-Germain, a philosophy professor at the Université du Québec à Montréal, wrote a rabid essay denouncing the gentlemanly efforts of Quebec's politicians over fifty years to negotiate their way towards independence: "From an historical point of view, the efforts of the humblest Ursuline nun in Trois Rivières to save the French language after the Conquest was worth more for the survival of our people than the whole light brigade of *Bloc québécois* 'revolutionaries' who went to Ottawa to earn a federal pension."[15] He was also scathing about other French-speaking minorities in North America. "At an Acadian cultural festival, you have to imagine the innocent outrages committed on the corpse of the French language by the descendants of deportees. It would almost be better to hear them speak English than prolong the torture."[16] Such *hauteur* can exasperate other activists. A prominent nationalist writer, Jacques Dufresne, who regards Wikipedia as a veiled device to impose the Anglo-Saxon outlook on the world, panned Saint-Germain's book, calling him a "troublemaker."[17]

A Sense of Family

Another feature of Quebec politics has been the kindness that political opponents can show to one another behind the scenes. Cynics might dismiss this as clubby; others might see it as only natural in a relatively small society; but many Quebeckers are not aware of it or take it for granted. Shortly after the 1970 October Crisis, Pierre Bourgault, a pioneer of the independence movement, lost his job as editor of a weekly news magazine. René Lévesque, who shunned "revolutionaries" like Bourgault, did nothing to help. It was the Liberal premier, Robert Bourassa, an old schoolmate of Bourgault's, who offered him work translating official documents at the Government of Quebec publications office. Even Lester Pearson, until recently prime minister of the country that Bourgault wanted to dismember, considered asking him to translate his memoirs.[18] In 2002, the funeral of Louis Laberge, a sometimes fiery trade union leader who had skewered the entire political class in his time and once spent three months in jail for organizing an illegal strike, was attended by fifteen hundred people, including every prominent politician of the time.[19]

Such crossings of party lines are larger than personal ties overcoming political rivalries. There is a strong sense of family in Quebec combined with a sentimental streak that can surprise outsiders. In January 2016, for example, the husband of the singer Céline Dion was given a state funeral. In July 2018, when Quebec's most famous theatre director Robert Lepage had two productions cancelled for perceived insensitivity to people of African and Indigenous descent, most editorial writers and every major political party came to his defence. A deep sense of history also pervades the political class. In April 2005, the remains of a famous nun (Saint Marguerite Bourgeoys, who founded the Congréga- tion de Notre Dame, a Catholic teaching order, in the seventeenth century) were transferred from the community's motherhouse in the city to a small chapel in Old Montreal. The mayor of the city and two ministers (one federal and one provincial) led the cortège on foot.[20] And in November 2018, Quebec's new premier – not his minister of culture – held a press conference to announce the discovery of remnants of the 1693 wooden ramparts of Quebec City.

As in many open societies, there has been a significant amount of political corruption at the provincial and municipal levels, but the media and courts have unearthed it successfully. Some of it has been used to fund political activity illicitly rather than to line the pockets of the guilty parties. In 2016, the first English-speaking mayor of Montreal since 1912, Michael Applebaum, was convicted of taking thirty thousand dollars in bribes to finance municipal party expenses. Although there is no excusing it, such cheating may be a by-product of the toughest election financing laws in the world. Under Quebec law, no individual or corporation is allowed to donate more than $100 a year to a political party or candidate, except in an election year, when an extra $100 contribution is permitted. In March 2017, the small *indépendantiste* party Québec solidaire was criticized for using a loophole in the law to provide $1,200 *from its own resources* to two candidates vying for party leadership posts. And in July 2018 the media billionaire Pierre Karl Péladeau was fined $27,600 for retiring a $135,000 campaign debt – incurred when he ran for the leadership of the Parti québécois – from his own pocket rather than from citizen contributions.[21]

All of that is the good news. The bad news is that political debates in Quebec suffer from an unnecessary degree of exaggeration, posturing, pettiness, and passion. A large part of that is explained by Quebec's French heritage. In the words of the nineteenth-century historian Jules Michelet, "We gossip, we quarrel, we expend our energy in words: we use strong language, and fly into great rages over the smallest of subjects." His contemporary, Hippolyte Taine, tried to put a positive face on this trait: "All that the Frenchman desires is to provoke in himself and in others a bubbling of agreeable ideas." On the other side of the Channel, Keir Hardie, a founder of the British Labour Party, described his compatriots as "solid and not given to chasing bubbles."[22] But a more important cause of the sometimes-aggravating antics in Quebec politics is an electoral system that distorts political realities, misreads the public will, and dampens interest in public debate. The most important fact about Quebec's political history is that under a more rational electoral system (proportional representation) there would never have been an *indépendantiste* government, as the main party supporting it never received more than 50 per cent of the vote.

Trudeau and Lévesque

Like most societies, Quebec is an array of disparate communities that converge like tectonic plates at election time. Age brings a particular outlook. Quebeckers over fifty still remember Pierre Elliott Trudeau, Canadian prime minister (for all but nine months) from 1968 to 1984, and René Lévesque, his Quebec counterpart from 1976 to 1985. It would be hard to imagine two more dissimilar politicians. Born into wealth in Montreal's genteel Outremont neighbourhood and a graduate of Harvard and the London School of Economics, Trudeau was cosmopolitan, stylish, highbrow, and contemptuous of smaller intellects. Lévesque was from a small town in the Gaspé Region and had always had to work for a living. Short, dishevelled, and a chain smoker, he had also been abroad, as a journalist in the Second World War, but remained true to his humble beginnings. In the words of a biographer, "[Lévesque] was the personification of Quebec and its carnal attachment to the Laurentian soil; [Trudeau] represented Canada, the country-continent open to every form of hope." According to Claude Charron, a former *indépendantiste* minister, "Lévesque was the man all of us knew we were, to some degree. Trudeau was the man we all would like to have been."[23]

For voters who knew these two men, the chasm they represented remains at the heart of the political debate. Trudeau wanted French speakers to feel at home in the whole of Canada and resented those who would keep them quarantined in Quebec. Lévesque charted what he thought was a more realistic course: protecting a culture that was under siege even within its own boundaries. Both men were deeply loved. When the train carrying Trudeau's body back to Montreal passed slowly through the station at Alexandria, Ontario, in 2000, journalists heard a strange squeaking noise. It was the sound of hundreds of respectful hands touching the carriage as it went by.[24] In 1977, on his way home from a late-night dinner party, Lévesque ran over a homeless man lying in the street. In the days that followed, there was more sympathy for Lévesque than the man he killed. Yet, in the end, many *Québécois* saw Trudeau as highly divisive while, for most, Lévesque could do no wrong. Even English speakers, deeply worried about their future, listened to him with respect and admiration. My mother, who spared no adjectives for those *indépendantistes* who delighted in sowing fear, would smile impishly after hearing Lévesque explain his positions on television in earthy, colloquial English.

New Voices

For younger Quebeckers, Trudeau and Lévesque may as well have lived in the nineteenth century. Their elders still think of the Parti québécois (the main independence party) as "progressive"; but millennials associate it with the "heartless" austerity programs that the two major parties have imposed since the early 1990s. (See chapter 4.) Not surprisingly, many of them now support Québec solidaire, a small party that has moved to the forefront of the political stage very quickly and distinguished itself by its anti-populist positions, like opposing the proposed Charter of Quebec Values in 2014 and voting against a large government subsidy for a privately run hockey arena in Quebec City. Its leadership bridges the generations very cleverly. One of its two co-spokespeople is Gabriel Nadeau-Dubois, aged twenty-eight, who was one of the leaders of the student strike of 2012 opposing higher tuition fees. The "Maple Spring" now seems like a footnote in the province's history, but at the time it provoked an outpouring of anger, hyperbole, anarchism, and police violence reflecting the deep passions that lie just below the orderly surface of Quebec politics. Although it was by no means the "historic" watershed that its leaders imagined and resulted in a mere postponement of higher tuition fees, it contradicted the notion that Quebec millennials were politically apathetic and revealed a profound contempt for the established political class or, at least, for traditional political arguments.

Québec solidaire's other co-spokesperson (the party abhors the idea of having "leaders") is a fifty-five-year-old veteran community organizer named Manon Massé. In an image-conscious age, she attracted ribald commentary in 2014 for refusing to shave her moustache before being photographed for her election posters. More significantly, from an early age she wanted to become a Roman Catholic priest. When told that this would be impossible, she decided to pour her energies into other forms of public service. Her idealism is obvious and contagious. Her party proposes a Constituent Assembly that would write a new constitution for Quebec, with the important proviso that sitting members of the National Assembly would not be part of it. "We don't want professional politicians dominating the process," she told me. "Some mainstream nationalists have questioned this and want sovereignists to run the show, but we think that Quebeckers of all points of view should be in charge."

She is also sensitive to history and to others. "We are just as interested in protecting the cultures of the First Nations as we are in defending ours. In fact, their way of life is under even greater threat. And isn't it ironic that we, the *Québécois*, the first 'immigrants' here, have waited almost five hundred years to consider sharing community resources and protecting nature? The First Nations have been talking about these two things for ten thousand years." She is also clear about her basic beliefs. "Who needs to earn more than $1 million or even $500,000 a year? Speaking personally rather than for the party, I think that any income above that should be taxed 100 per cent."[25] In May 2018, her party chose her as its candidate for premier in the October 2018 elections. She ran a strong campaign, tripling the number of her party's seats in the National Assembly, and putting climate change for the first time at the heart of the political debate.

The Electoral System

For most of the twentieth century, Quebec had only two major parties: a liberal and a conservative one, leaving very little choice between voting *rouge* or *bleu*.* That changed in November 1976 when René Lévesque brought his Parti québécois to power for the first time. The cause of independence cut across left-right lines, but most *péquistes*† saw themselves as a progressive alternative to the establishment Liberals, and in their eighteen years in power (1976–85, 1994–2003, 2013–14) introduced a series of measures like election financing laws and subsidized day care that set Quebec apart from the rest of Canada. For a while,

---

* Red (for liberal) or blue (for conservative).
† Supporters of the Parti québécois (PQ).

conservatives had nowhere to go, but their impatience with high taxes and borrowing and the social impact of mass immigration eventually bubbled up in the form of a new party, the Action démocratique du Québec (ADQ) and its successor the Coalition Avenir Québec (CAQ).

Voters now have a choice between four sizeable parties (the Liberals, the CAQ, the Parti québécois, and Québec solidaire), creating strains on an electoral system once built on a two-party system. The "first past the post" Westminster model gave Canada ten years of government by a Conservative Party (2006–15) that never won more than 39 per cent of the popular vote. Quebec already faced anomalies under a system that gives rural voters greater weight than urban ones (because of the smaller populations of rural ridings). In 1998, the new Liberal leader Jean Charest won the highest share of the vote but had to sit in opposition for five years because his opponent Lucien Bouchard of the Parti québécois won a larger number of seats, many of them rural.

The system is now even more unpredictable, given the number of horses in the race. In the 2014 election, Québec solidaire won nearly 8 per cent of the popular vote, which in a system of proportional representation would have assured it 9 of the 125 seats in the National Assembly; instead, they eked out 3. The Liberals won 70 seats instead of the 52 they would have had based purely on their share of the vote, and the CAQ should have won 7 more seats (29 instead of 22), making them a natural partner in a coalition with the Liberals. Instead, there was no need for such cooperation, as the Liberals won a majority of seats with only a plurality of the vote. Four years of bickering between the Liberals and the CAQ could have been avoided and Quebeckers would have felt themselves more faithfully represented if the two centrist parties had joined forces. Québec solidaire could also have had a larger voice and its voters could have felt three times better than they did on election night and during the next four years. (See chapter 6.)

The dynamism of political opinion in Quebec does not prevent some nationalists from deploring the "apathy" of their fellow citizens or their focus on the "wrong" issues. In the words of one observer, "You'd think we were living in a gigantic hospital, the way the whole political debate seems to boil down to how to reduce the length of waiting times in the health service. As if an otherwise individualistic people had found a symbolic way of becoming a community again: through shared suffering."[26]

Fighting Poverty

That image is both amusing and appropriate because, despite differing views about other issues, the commitment of Quebeckers to maintaining a strong social safety net is deep and widespread, building upon the performance of Canada as a whole. Between 2000 and 2010, the proportion of poor families in Canada with children under five dropped by 62 per cent. This was the result of redistributive policies like automatic food allowances, the law on equity of salaries, bonuses for people with low wages, child allowances, and the creation of a system of low-cost childcare. The latter policy allowed tens of thousands of women to enter training or the job market, with the spectacular result of reducing the proportion of single mothers seeking welfare by 60 per cent between 1990 and 2010.[27]

If Canada has done well on the social policy front, Quebec has done even better and, internationally, is second only to Scandinavia in narrowing the gap between rich and poor. Over the last fifteen years, poverty in Quebec has dropped steadily (from a peak of 18.5 per cent in 1997), reflected in a persistent drop in the number of people seeking welfare.[28] Does this mean that Quebec has done as much as it can? Certainly not. In 2011, 842,000 Quebeckers still did not have the means to lead a decent life.* And in 2013, 228,000 Quebec households were spending more than 50 per cent of their income on rent.[29] For people in this situation, an inconvenience anywhere else – like a refrigerator breaking down – becomes a

---

* This means that they could not afford the minimum level of nutrition, housing, clothing, transport, and small assets (telephone, furniture, small electrical appliances, sporting goods, entertainment, etc.) necessary for a reasonably balanced life.

crisis. Women are particularly affected, heading all the groups that are typically poor: one-parent households, the handicapped, First Peoples, and immigrants. Two-thirds of minimum-wage earners are women.

Poverty is not just a statistical matter. The blood and saliva of underprivileged ten-year-olds already predict high risks of heart disease and respiratory illnesses later in life. In Canada, poor children under the age of seventeen enter hospital 80 per cent more often than those who are better off.[30] For this reason, one doctor at St. Michael's Hospital in Toronto asks new patients how much they earn even before looking into their medical histories. "Raising the incomes of poor people will have at least as much of a positive effect on their health as all the medicines I can prescribe for them," says Dr. Gary Bloch. "For me, poverty itself is an illness."[31] Often, he has his staff help patients apply for government income supplements, the effects of which can show up quite quickly in their health.

A more bracing and surprising verdict – given his politics – is that of James Hughes, a former deputy minister of social development in New Brunswick and NDP* candidate in Montreal in the 2015 federal election: "Ronald Reagan's claim that 'the best social program is a job' is largely accurate. For those who are able and have the opportunity, employment has proven from the Depression to today to be one of the best cures for poverty. Welfare has proven to be the opposite, a toxin with paralytic qualities capable of locking people in a state of poverty."[32]

Yet, no amount of economic growth or wage improvement will keep everyone out of poverty. For short or longer periods, because of economic change, geographic location, disability, and the lack of appropriate skills, a significant number of people will depend on the generosity of the rest of society. Quebec has stood out in understanding this basic point. While other large Canadian provinces started cutting back on the welfare state in the 1990s, Quebec maintained and increased social spending, confirming its position as the only social democratic society in North

---

* The NDP (New Democratic Party) is a nominally socialist federal party.

America.[33] Once again, the lasting influence of Catholic values may have played a role.

Impressive Progress ...

Quebec stands out not only for the level but also for the nature of its social spending. While Canada has a well-deserved reputation as a liberal society, social policy varies across provinces as widely as among rich countries as a whole, from the relative parsimony of the United States to the full-blown protections of Sweden and Denmark. Some scholars draw a distinction between "punitive" and "activating" programs, that is, those that focus on keeping the number of recipients to a minimum by making welfare highly conditional and those who use it to help people re-enter the workforce through training programs and job counselling. Quebec is firmly in the "activist" camp. It also focusses on families with children who may become poor and reconciling work and family obligations through affordable day care and generous parental leave programs.[34]

Intelligent social programs can bring a range of benefits. For example, nothing is more important for preventing poverty than early-learning programs. Job training has nowhere near the same impact – or economic rate of return – as proper childhood education. Quebec's subsidized childcare program leads the country in access to physical facilities: 50 per cent of families, compared with about 26 per cent in Canada as a whole. And the program allowed a larger number of women to enter the workforce than anywhere else in North America. One result was that the number of single mothers on welfare dropped by more than half in twelve years.* Economists estimate that the cost of the Quebec childcare program ($2.2 billion in 2014) was completely recovered by the influx of women into the labour market, which added to government revenues (through higher income and sales taxes) and savings on tax credits, welfare payments,

---

* From 99,000 in 1996 to 45,000 in 2008.

and other social benefits. But more work needs to be done. Obviously, the quality of early-learning programs is just as important as the number of children enrolled. Yet, according to a 2010 evaluation, only a quarter of Quebec's 1,574 day-care centres were judged "good" and 40 per cent did not even meet the minimum standard.[35]

... But Much Remains to be Done

Although Quebec has taken a national lead in childcare, in other aspects of social policy its performance is not very different from that of the rest of Canada – which itself is nothing to brag about. In 2000, the World Health Organization ranked Canada's health system thirtieth in the world – ahead of the United States (thirty-seventh) but well behind France (first), the United Kingdom (eighteenth), and Sweden (twenty-third). In 2007, the Commonwealth Fund placed Canada sixth among seven countries (including France, the United Kingdom, Finland, and Sweden) on access to health services. On coordination of care, it was at the bottom, alongside the United States.[36] In 2011, Canada spent more on health than most other rich countries but had close to the worst results.[37]

Yet, in many respects, Quebec did even worse. In fact, the province has consistently been one of the poorest-performing health systems in the country. In 2009, despite its having more doctors per capita than Ontario and Canada generally, 27 per cent of the population did not have a family doctor (the figure was even higher in Montreal), compared with 15 per cent in the whole of Canada. Waiting times in hospital emergency wards averaged seventeen hours compared with the official target of twelve hours, which was already loose. (In Ontario, the target was eight hours.) Quebeckers waited 65 days longer than other Canadians (225 days) to have a colonoscopy. More than 18,000 patients waited a year for physiotherapy.[38] And, in 2012, there were 225,600 medical accidents and errors in Quebec, resulting in 123 deaths and another 121 people with permanent injuries.[39]

To cite one prominent critic, "This has gone on for so long that it is regarded as normal and does not provoke revolt or indignation. Yet, the way patients are treated seems inadmissible to me. In the morning, when I enter some of our larger hospitals, I have the impression of finding myself in a hospital in Eastern Europe before the collapse of the Berlin Wall. We should be ashamed of the situation."[40]

To balance this gloom, it needs to be said that Quebec's health system is generally successful in treating real emergencies and that more than 80 per cent of patients routinely praise the quality of care once they have been admitted into the system. A 2017 survey by the conservative Fraser Institute established that Canadians are treated for cancer treatment within 3.2 weeks of diagnosis (compared with 21.2 weeks for all kinds of treatment) and that the proportion of people in Quebec awaiting treatment in general (1.2 per cent) was the lowest in Canada.[41]

But structural and policy problems still need attention. According to David Levine, a former Quebec junior minister of health and hospital CEO in Ottawa, Quebec has an "inefficient, hospital-centred system that is not responding to the overall needs of the population." Hospitals are also managed differently. In Ontario, well-paid CEOs are fully responsible for results. "In Quebec, it is hard to determine who is responsible for the institution as there is so much intervention by government and the regional agencies in the daily managing of the hospital, and there is a culture where nothing can be done without permission." Levine worried that the 2015 health system reforms would complicate the situation further by promoting even more centralization.[42]

Strengthening the Health System

While other rich countries have adapted their systems, there have been no significant changes to Canada's health legislation since 1984. Hence, a bias towards hospital care at the expense of ambulatory or home services remains in place. Nor do decision makers have the authority to spend public resources wisely, and outcomes are rarely assessed. In Levine's words, "In our highly centralized system, a culture has developed that is opposed to performance evaluation. And, in fact, our system favours no adaptation at all in a context of constant change, initiative, innovation, and the pursuit of excellence."[43]

Quebec's health system employs 290,000 people (including 16,700 doctors and 106,900 nurses and other professionals) spread across three hundred hospitals and other medical institutions and two thousand clinics and doctors' offices. It accounts for 10 per cent of Quebec's GDP and 13 per cent of employment. No other sector of activity or enterprise is as important or complex. Hence, there are no quick and easy solutions for improving the system. At the same time, no other reform is as important for translating Quebec's renowned solidarity into concrete results.[44]

Conservative economists have long complained that Canada is one of the few countries on earth (including Cuba and North Korea) that exclude the private sector from health services. Right-wing politicians have also asked why Quebeckers "have the right to buy two BMWs whenever they want but not to spend their own money on health care." Centrists, too, are now inclined to wonder why Canada should be so purist when other Western countries with a deep commitment to a universal health system, like France and the United Kingdom, have allowed a role for the private sector: introducing clear rules for private clinics, permitting doctors to work in public hospitals and have a private practice on the side, making it easier for people to buy private health insurance, and permitting private practitioners to borrow public infrastructure (generating revenue for the public system).

Although Quebec has allowed some exceptions to the Canada Health Act by authorizing private-sector medical imaging and minor surgery (like knee replacement and cataract operations), its politicians have been reluctant to go much further and, in any case, are prevented from doing so under federal law. Yet, public opinion appears to be running ahead of elected officials. Successive surveys commissioned by the Montreal Economic Institute (an admittedly conservative body) show that almost two in three Quebeckers support establishing a parallel system for those who can afford faster care, provided it does not weaken the public system. In this case, as in others, Quebec is quite different from the rest of Canada.[45]

Other Challenges

Getting the current health system to perform better is one thing. Gearing it up to deal with new challenges before they get out of hand is just as important. In 2011, more than a million young Canadians were living with symptoms of mental illness. Yet, only a quarter of them were receiving any treatment at all, let alone an adequate one, despite the fact that 70 per cent of cases of depression, anxiety, and psychosis start early in life and 150,000 young Canadians attempt suicide each year. Quebec faces a particular challenge in that respect, with 1,100 suicides per year, three times the number killed in road accidents.[46] Once again, Canada's failure to be proactive is due largely to a hospital-oriented system more adept at handling emergencies (using sedation, stomach pumping, and surgery) than preventing them. In the view of specialists, such an approach is clearly short sighted. In 2010, Canada spent $3,300 per person on health services but only $245 on mental health, even though mental-health problems cost the economy an estimated $50 billion per year.[47] Another challenge is Alzheimer's disease, which affects 500,000 Canadians – a number that will triple by 2038. If Canada and Quebec continue to manage the disease late through hospitalization and nursing care, the economic burden will rise. Early intervention, including physical exercise, can slow or prevent the disease, saving up to $50 billion over thirty years.[48]

Beyond health services, Quebec's broader system of social protection has also been the subject of numerous studies and complaints, sparking successive waves of reforms. The pace of change, in turn, has been a source of grievance among a wide range of advocacy groups trying to keep the government on its toes. In February 2016, Virginie Larivière, spokesperson for the Collectif pour un Québec sans pauvreté (Collective for a Quebec without poverty), complained that she had been at the Collectif for only two and half years and was already into her third round of reform of social services. "They are hounding the poor!" she lamented. She knew that public opinion was divided on the subject, with radio talk shows denouncing all welfare recipients as "lazy" or "crooks." But "no one is immune from perhaps having to seek government help one day. No one."[49]

A Guaranteed Annual Income?

One reason for the frequency of reforms is the sheer number of overlapping programs and the need to curb apparent waste. For example, in 2016, about eleven thousand able-bodied young people were claiming welfare in Quebec.[50] The search for better solutions has given rise to a debate about introducing a guaranteed annual income that would roll a number of support programs into one and target those who are most in need. In the last ten years, the idea has gained strength on both the left and right as a means of enshrining the "rights" of poor people and simplifying access to government help (popular on the left) while eliminating duplication and unnecessary staffing and paperwork (dear to the right). But the challenge is in the details and, so far, the idea has not proved popular.

In June 2016, Switzerland was the first country to hold a referendum on the subject and the idea was voted down by three-quarters of the voters.[51] The Socialist Party candidate in France's April 2017 presidential elections also campaigned for a guaranteed income and was defeated ignominiously. Finland decided against expanding its small-scale experiment in April 2018, while a month later Italy announced that it would be introducing a "citizens' income" without piloting it, the first country to do so. But, while the idea has become more respectable among economists in recent years, it is far from new in Quebec. Forty years ago, René Lévesque speculated that a minimum guaranteed income could prove the ultimate solution for focussing public resources on those most in need while safeguarding the incentive to work.[52] And Quebec's former minister of employment and social solidarity, a personal supporter of the concept, launched a public consultation on the matter in December 2016.[53] (For further discussion of this topic, see chapter 6.)

Public-private partnerships are also a possible solution. In November 2015, the Quebec government said that it was prepared to consider issuing "social-impact bonds" to fund public-interest programs operated by the private sector. Such "bonds" – which would guarantee a financial rate of return based on meeting agreed targets – are still at an early stage of development. Only forty projects exist in the world, including thirty in the United Kingdom and eight in the United States. Ontario is considering using this approach in finding jobs for young people, housing and counselling street people suffering from mental illness, and keeping young ex-detainees out of prison.[54]

In meeting its social obligations, Quebec will need to build on the comity of its political culture and the deep commitment of most of its citizens to fairness and compassion, amply reflected in the narrow differences on social policy in the October 2018 election.* These aspects of solidarity are strengths that many Quebeckers are proud of. But neither will be enough to sustain progress in reducing poverty if economic challenges are not taken seriously as well.

---

* For example, the Coalition Avenir Québec, the most conservative party, promised to reduce medical salaries so as to free up funds for higher priorities in the health system.

4

Efficiency

Éric Duhaime is now a radio commentator in Quebec City, but he once worked for Mario Dumont, leader of the Action démocratique du Québec, a conservative political party. One day, on his way out of a parliamentary committee meeting, Duhaime saw the head of one of the province's largest unions rip into his boss. The unionist accused Dumont of being "in the pay of the rich" for supporting a government bill that would simplify subcontracting. Dumont shrugged off the insult and slipped away, without pointing out that the union boss made twice as much as he did and was about to be driven to one of Quebec City's finest restaurants by a chauffeur funded by union members. Dumont would drive home in a minivan paid for from his own pocket. As for Duhaime, with an MA in public administration and ten years' experience as an economist and political aide, he made less than a receptionist at the union head office and only a fraction of some union leaders' expense accounts.

His verdict was sharp: "If only union leaders preached by example, led a modest life, and stayed close to the people they claim to defend! But what really takes the cake is to see these same people denounce the concentration of wealth in the hands of the 1% while claiming that they are part of the 99%. What hypocrisy! At some point, progressive people have to realize that their precious union allies ARE the 1%! We are a long way from the supposed defence of widows and orphans."[1]

The Economy in a New Light

Duhaime is not the only conservative economist in Quebec to move from muttering under his breath to venting his frustration out loud. Joanne Marcotte, whose 2006 documentary *L'Illusion tranquille* (The quiet illusion) targeted some of the province's cherished beliefs, started her 2011 book *Pour en finir avec le gouvernemaman* (Putting an end to the nanny state) with a quotation from the nineteenth-century French economist Frédéric Bastiat (1801–50): "The State is a huge invention through which everybody tries to live at someone else's expense."[2] I smiled when I saw this as, twenty years before, when I headed the World Bank office in Western Africa, I used a Bastiat fable to illustrate the dangers of monopolies. (Bastiat imagined a country in which candle makers convinced the king to outlaw windows so as to increase their market.) I also thought of that fable shortly after, when I read about three small maple syrup producers facing hundreds of thousands of dollars in penalties for selling outside the provincial cartel.

Is it fair to compare Quebec to West Africa? Obviously not, if we focus on their overall levels of economic and social development. But, psychologically, certain parallels exist. In French-speaking Africa, many people prefer monopolies to open markets. In Quebec, public ownership is so widespread that the very use of the word "monopoly" is taken as a symptom of being right wing. In Africa, workers' rights are codified in a book as thick as the Bible (as they still are in France). The notion that workers' rights are no longer very fragile in most Western countries and that they need to be balanced against those of employers, consumers, and taxpayers seems heretical in Quebec, as it does in Africa and France.

Quebec and French West Africa also share an important cultural heritage: the French habit of intervening in detailed economic decision making (*dirigisme*). Two years ago, in the Paris neighbourhood where I live, a popular grocery store was shut down because the local authorities decided the chain already had enough outlets nearby and forced it to surrender the space to another chain store. Across France, shops can only reduce prices on dates dictated by the state. In Quebec, self-imposed restrictions fly in the face of commercial reason. It is only recently that car dealers in the province opened on Saturdays and they are still closed on Sundays. How many working people can shop for a car during the week?

Most French and *Québécois* suspect the rich and expect the state to be generous to those who are not. (Africans do not have strong views on the subject, as few are wealthy and governments have trouble providing even basic services.)

And finally, like African governments, Quebec may have become too dependent on "foreign aid," in its case the equalization payments that it has received from Ottawa for decades as a "have-not" province.

That said, market-friendly economists in Quebec can sound like evangelical temperance campaigners screaming from a pulpit. Some of their critiques are worth considering, even when they are expressed flamboyantly. Others are simply unfair and ignore the strong political and social consensus underlying many of Quebec's choices. To sort the wheat from the chaff, we need to look at the province's achievements over the last fifty years.

Fifty Years of Progress

When Pierre Vallières wrote his controversial book *The White Niggers of North America* (1968), he was not completely wide of the mark. In 1960, the average *Québécois* spent only ten years in school and earned only half as much as English speakers, numbers remarkably similar to the situation of African Americans vis-à-vis whites at the time.[3] That changed as a result of the Quiet Revolution (1960–6), when the Liberal government of Jean Lesage shrugged off the inaction and paternalism of the Maurice Duplessis era (1944–59) and gave the Quebec state a leading role in economic and social development. Few people are aware of just how dramatically Quebec changed after that.

Quebeckers in their late twenties now have the same amount of schooling as young people in Ontario and slightly more than in the rest of Canada and the United States (fifteen years). Young Quebeckers also score near the top of international competency tests in mathematics, reading, and the sciences. If Quebec were a country, it would have ranked among the world's top five performers in science in a 2017 international student assessment test.[4] Given the direct relationship between schooling and jobs, there should be little surprise that there has been a marked improvement in youth employment in the province.[5]

Despite major differences in economic performance – especially in the 1980s when Quebec suffered a long series of labour disputes – over a period of six decades (1945–2007) per capita income grew faster in Quebec than in Ontario, its richer neighbour. In absolute terms, incomes remained higher in Ontario, but here, too, at the end of the period, taking the cost of living into account, Quebec was 92 per cent as well off.[6]

Quebec's achievements came at a cost. Pierre Fortin of the Université du Quebec à Montréal, one of the province's most prominent and engaging analysts, suggests that the two premiers who borrowed most heavily, Robert Bourassa (1970–76 and 1985–94) and Jacques Parizeau (1994–6), were frustrated economists. Growing up under Maurice Duplessis, who was in office for seventeen years, they were astounded that he refused to use one of the most obvious levers of economic development, borrowing, to foster a better future. It was two lawyers – Lucien Bouchard (1996–2001) and Jean Charest (2003–12) – who began the difficult work of bringing Quebec's debt burden under control.[7]

In 2013, Quebec had the highest government debt in Canada ($22,000 per capita), equivalent to 49 per cent of GDP. (Ontario's was 37 per cent and that of the state of New York just 12 per cent.)[8] In addition, Quebec's personal income tax rates are among the highest in North America, with combined federal-provincial rates approaching 50 per cent for the highest earners. In North America, only California, Hawaii, and New York have higher taxes.[9] Partly as a result, for about ten years growth in per capita income, employment, and private investment in Quebec stalled.[10] Yet, concern about debt and taxes was not widespread outside the business community and the relatively well off. Time and again in public surveys, most respondents did not believe that tax reform should be a government priority. One reason for that is that 40 per cent of Quebeckers do not pay any income tax.

New Challenges

Now, Quebec faces an additional challenge. Between 1981 and 2005, its population grew by only 16 per cent, compared with 30 per cent in Canada and the United States and 42 per cent in Ontario.[11] As a result, by 2050 Quebec will have the third oldest population in the Western world, after Italy and Japan.[12] Certainly, Quebec's situation reflects a broader pattern in North America, but the drop in the birth rate was sharper and faster than anywhere else, with the result that the ratio of workers to retirees has dropped from seven to one in 1986 to three to one in 2010 and is expected to slip further to two to one by 2020.[13] By 2040, a quarter of all Quebeckers will be over sixty-five.[14] Already, between 2014 and 2017, progress in reducing hospital waiting times was wiped out by the higher number of older patients needing urgent care.[15] These facts have profound implications for designing public policy and promoting a social consensus during the next ten to fifteen years.

One important consequence is that governments will almost certainly have to run steady budget surpluses so as to afford the increasing health costs associated with an aging population. Raising taxes or borrowing to fund them will simply add to the burden that future generations already face in maintaining the current level of services. Another implication is that Quebec must do all it can to increase the productivity of its shrinking working-age population. Yet, investment in education dropped from 30 per cent of Quebec's budget in 1981 to 23 per cent in 2011, crowded out by expenditures on health (now 50 per cent of the budget). As a result, teachers' salaries are lower than in other provinces and school maintenance has been woefully neglected. Yet, the educational challenge remains high. Each day, one hundred young people drop out of school in Quebec and

31 per cent (36 per cent in the case of of boys) do not complete high school before the age of twenty, putting Quebec behind all other Canadian provinces and rich countries.[16]

The Case for Efficiency

Making room for crucial social investments without raising debt and taxes will require tight management of all government spending and a more vigorous economy, which in turn should yield higher public revenues. Yet, many Quebeckers regard efficiency as a dirty word. There was a public outcry in November 2014 when the Liberal government raised day-care fees for families earning more than $150,000 from $7 to $20 per day. The change saved only $300 million on a budget of $2.4 billion and the day-care program remained one of the most generous in Canada.[17]

Sometimes, saving money can go hand in hand with doing things better. Claude Castonguay, who designed Quebec's public health system, thinks that evaluating the performance of Quebec's hospitals on a regular basis would make the health system more dynamic, while also saving hundreds of millions of dollars per year. (In 2012, hospitals absorbed half of the total health budget, more than the entire spending of the Ministry of Education or any other public service.) Yet, at the moment, all hospitals are treated the same, with no effort to reward efficiency and good service. In the United Kingdom, despite initial resistance to the idea, hospitals are graded independently against a range of criteria and the results are made public online. Such evaluation contributes to the spread of sound practices, allowing the government to reward good performers (by letting them carry budget savings over to the next year) and identify institutions needing more attention and help. "In all these systems, emphasis is put on transparency. Staff at our Ministry of Health are hermits by comparison," says Castonguay.[18]

Such reforms are not just necessary now. They will need to be continued and broadened if future governments are to balance the needs of current and future generations and invest in services for an aging population without undermining the incentives and rewards for those still working. In that respect, the size of Quebec's government is a definite issue, with one employee for every seventeen people, compared with one to twenty-two in Ontario. More strikingly, Quebec has more staff in its health and social services (272,454) than Ontario (236,448) even though Ontario has two-thirds more people.[19]

Quebec's crown corporations also have fat. In 2017, the state alcohol monopoly (Société des alcools du Québec, or SAQ) had more employees than the Liquor Control Board of Ontario (LCBO), even though the latter's sales were almost twice as high.[20] In 2018, the SAQ president earned $419,704 – more than double the salary of Quebec's premier.[21]

Quebec spends three times more than Ontario subsidizing some of its businesses: $3.4 billion, or 1.2 per cent of its GDP in 2014. (This issue will be discussed at greater length below.)

All these opportunities for efficiency are within the government's control. Others need to be pursued through public education and, in some cases, by interfering with the "acquired rights" of vested interests. If trade unions have been instrumental in improving working conditions over the last century and are still important in ensuring that wages keep pace with corporate profits, the bad habits that some unions have fostered are a barrier to economic and social progress. The construction industry, in particular, is rife with cost padding, corruption, and what economists describe as "featherbedding."

Except for small projects like home renovation, construction workers in Quebec must be hired from five certified unions representing twenty-six specialized skills in thirteen designated regions. (In Ontario, there are only six recognized trades and builders can work anywhere they want.) That means that employers must hire extra people just to respect an outdated hierarchy of skills and workers have trouble moving from one region to another. For example, if ironworking were classified as one building trade rather than three, contractors might be able to hire fewer workers and reduce the cost of public contracts, which are at least 10 per cent more expensive than they should be.[22] One does not need to be indifferent to workers' rights to see such practices as an unfair raid on public money at the expense of the community as a whole.

Promoting the Right Kind of Growth

Government cost cutting by itself, however, cannot safeguard necessary programs. A more reliable course is to promote economic growth, which in turn should strengthen public revenues. But, like efficiency, growth is often frowned upon in progressive circles. This suspicion is sound if it focusses on economic activity that wastes natural resources, endangers precious flora and fauna, and pours greenhouse gasses into the atmosphere. But switching off the engines of human enterprise and invention is not the way to protect the environment. Harnessing them to a better set of policies and rewarding ingenious solutions would be much more promising.

Just as international development economists have promoted "fair" growth that benefits the largest number of poor people in developing countries, the challenge for Quebec is to pursue "green" growth that will increase the total amount of public and private resources available to society without exacting irreversible costs. Expanding the range of products using recycled materials, pushing hard against the current limits of energy efficiency, and developing technologies for cutting CO_2 emissions more effectively will all prove financially rewarding and foster growth that everyone can be proud of. In contrast, aiming at no growth or even negative growth would make social policy all the harder by forcing governments to decide who should get fewer public benefits (rather than more) and threatening the future of social programs that Quebeckers now take for granted.

How to achieve growth that is both "green" and "fair" is of course a matter of debate. (For a discussion of climate change, see the next chapter.) Like their counterparts everywhere, Quebec economists can be irreverent and radical. Why – asks one – doesn't Quebec sell its hydropower directly to foreign markets rather than "cheaply" in the form of aluminum (90 per cent of the cost of which is electricity),[23] as if the jobs created were insignificant or a government would shut down an important industry to test his theory. Another economist would "privatize" the government's liquor agency (the SAQ) by selling it to the highest bidder, as if a private monopoly would function better than a state one.[24] Such speculation is in the nature of the economist's craft, questioning the obvious and sometimes caricaturing the present so as to push the boundaries of policy in a more sensible direction.

It could be argued that good public policy is even more important in a mature market economy like Quebec's than in a less advanced one or even a "command" economy like Cuba's and North Korea's where governments make all the important decisions. That is because, in a rich country, good policy builds on market structures that are already directing resources to things that people value. Policy makers must also recognize their limitations, as most economies do not control all the forces shaping them.

Quebec used to produce 90 per cent of one of the world's most useful industrial materials. Now, there is no market for it at all and no one misses it, except perhaps in the small town of Asbestos. Over the last fifty years, there has been a major shift in the US population from the northeast to the southeast and southwest, with incalculable but presumably negative effects on Quebec's markets. Even the completion of the Saint Lawrence Seaway in 1959, which deprived Montreal of its status as the only large international port on the waterway, shaped the regional economy in ways that policy makers had little influence over. More recently, climate change has allowed Quebec to rival the US state of Maine as the world's largest producer of wild blueberries because of more stable spring weather in the province.[25]

But large swaths of the economy can still be affected by policy, with very definite effects on people's lives. Opposition to oil and gas development in Quebec, including fracking (the injection of liquid at high pressure into underground fissures to extract shale gas) will mean forgoing real opportunities for increasing incomes and public revenues just as surely as it will protect land and water quality. Good policy is about choice rather than the blind use of formulae. It is also about re-evaluating programs regularly to make certain they are standing the test of time. Protectionist measures that are politely referred to as "supply management" cost Canadian consumers of milk, cheese, eggs, and chickens $2.6 billion more than they would pay in an open market, representing a subsidy of $200,000 per farm and over-spending of about $300 per Canadian household.[26] Does it still make sense to prop up inefficient farms and, if so, wouldn't it be fairer to do so through direct government subsidies funded through a progressive tax system, rather than through prices at the supermarket that everyone pays regardless of their income? The subject of supply management arose during the last Quebec election as a result of US pressure to abolish it, but – given the importance of rural votes – the pros and cons of the system were never properly debated.

Improving Productivity

While individual economies will vary, one major issue now unites them: a general slowing of productivity improvements across rich countries and some large emerging ones as well. The International Monetary Fund estimates that, if labour and investment had remained as productive as before the 2008 financial crisis, the world's advanced economies would now be 5 per cent richer – the equivalent of adding an economy the size of Japan to the total. Because productivity growth is vital to improving living standards, this slowdown has led to widespread debate.[27] But one thing is certain. Productivity has been increasing even more slowly in Canada and Quebec than elsewhere, for a number of reasons, including the smaller size of the Canadian economy, the more modest scale of the average firm, and possibly the slower introduction of advanced technology. This fact makes it all the more urgent to introduce solutions to the parts of the puzzle that are clear. While economists may differ on the specifics and sequence of the remedies, there is now a broad consensus about what Quebec needs to do.

Between 1999 and 2014, economic growth in Quebec was roughly the same as in Ontario and the United States but per capita income increased faster because population growth was slower in Quebec.*[28] Hence, strictly speaking, the province "outperformed" the others. But this is an arithmetical result rather than something to boast about, as few successful economies aim at having a stagnant or declining population. Quebec's economic "success" is also the obverse side of the problems it is storing up because of its aging population. Nonetheless, Quebec's recent record is less dismal than many critics have surmised.

Quebec has also had a highly open economy with exports accounting for as much as 57 per cent of GDP and 30 per cent of all jobs (rising to 73 per cent in the case of manufacturing). This openness brings advantages but also requires Quebec to adapt quickly to international developments so as to keep positioning itself properly in the global division of labour. Rigid policies and structures become all the more costly in such an environment.[29]

Work Practices. How Quebeckers work is an obvious factor. Since 2000, the most striking change has been a major increase in women's participation in the Quebec workforce, resulting from family-friendly social policies. However, the number of hours worked is the lowest in North America (thirty-one per week in 2014) though still higher than in France (twenty-eight) and Germany (twenty-five).[30] But working "harder" is not the obvious answer to raising productivity and certainly not a popular one, as one former premier (Lucien Bouchard) learned in 2006 when he complained that Quebeckers worked less than people in Ontario and "infinitely less" than Americans. Instead,

---

* Quebec's growth was 30 per cent versus 33 per cent in Ontario and 32 per cent in the United States. Per capita income rose by 19 per cent in Quebec versus 15 per cent in the United States and 11 per cent in Ontario. Canada as a whole is not a good comparator because of the distorting effects of oil and gas production in some provinces.

Quebeckers will need to work "better." In an economy where 72 per cent of wealth now comes from producing services rather than goods, this means improving organizational structures and internal processes rather than just investing in better technology. Being open to change and seeing competition as a challenge rather than a threat are key to improving productivity.[31]

Immigration. Higher immigration by itself is not a solution to an aging population, except at a level that most people would find unacceptable. One study suggests that Canadian immigration would have to rise from 250,000 to 850,000 per year to have any perceptible effect on productivity, and all new arrivals would need to be between the ages of twenty and twenty-four. But immigration is essential for meeting skill shortages and potentially adding entrepreneurial energy where it is needed the most. Yet, Quebec struggles with absorbing newcomers into the economy, with immigrant unemployment four percentage points higher than for other Quebeckers. (In Ontario, the difference is just 1 per cent.) Even immigrants with a university degree are three times more likely to be out of work, perhaps in part because Quebec tries to attract French speakers. Few of them also speak English at a time when bilingualism is increasingly important, especially in the Montreal job market.[32]

Labour Policy. In July 2017, for the first time in over forty years, Quebec's general unemployment rate dropped below 6 per cent (to 5.8), leading to speculation that Quebec might soon suffer a labour shortage. Hailing this progress, Premier Philippe Couillard crowed that "our team took Quebec out of the economic doghouse and made it a powerhouse in Canada."[33] But the job figures were also a harbinger of new problems. Jean-Guy Côté, an economist working at the Institut de Québec, suggested that the government encourage older workers to stay on the job and remove obstacles preventing more immigrants from entering the workforce. "It's an open secret that Quebec has done less well than the rest of Canada in that department and it's going to become vital – socially, not just economically – that we do better."[34] In other provinces, for example, it is illegal to make previous work in Canada a condition of employment. Recognizing foreign professional qualifications will also become increasingly important.

Technical and Vocational Training. The province is already facing serious shortages of specialized labour (like welders, machinists, and electrical mechanics), which became a central issue of the October 2018 election. Eric Tetrault, president of the Association of Manufacturers and Exporters of Quebec, believes that such skill gaps are hampering Quebec's chances of profiting fully from the Canada–European Union trade agreement and the Trans-Pacific Partnership. In Tetrault's view, shortening vocational training programs (now as long as six years) and offering part-time training to people already employed could help correct such bottlenecks. He adds, "Parents need to get over the idea that vocational training is a dead end. Half of Germany's CEOs have risen from the ranks of technical staff."[35] Quebec must also take steps to battle adult illiteracy, as more than half of Quebeckers have varying degrees of difficulty reading.[36]

Tax Reform. As we have seen, Quebec's tax system sets it apart from most of the rest of North America. But its structure, not just its level, is problematical. Although down from a peak of 40 per cent of GDP in 2000, total Quebec taxes (now 37 per cent) are still three percentage points higher than the rich-country average (34 per cent) and five percentage points higher than in the rest of Canada. Only ten European countries charge more. Quebec also relies more heavily on personal income tax than most other rich countries. It is 50 per cent above the average for those countries and 22 per cent more than in the rest of Canada.* Corporate taxes, too, are 30 per cent higher than the rich-country average and consumption taxes are lower.†

The Organisation for Economic Co-operation and Development (OECD), which coordinates the policies of thirty-six advanced economies and is the source of these data, has concluded

---

* Concretely, in 2013, Quebeckers paid $6.5 billion more in income tax than their neighbours in Ontario, a province that has 60 per cent more people.

† Consumption taxes were 7.4 per cent in Quebec in 2013 compared with a rich-country average of 9.4 per cent.

that personal income taxes and corporate taxes can damage economic progress, while consumption (or sales) taxes are more
neutral in their impact. Quebec excels in the first two and has not
budged an inch in enhancing the share of sales taxes in the mix.

The fiscal economist Luc Godbout of the University of Sherbrooke recommends a shifting of Quebec's tax model away from
personal and corporate income tax towards greater reliance on
sales taxes. At the same time, he favours raising tax credits to
counter the effects of higher consumption taxes on the poor.[37]
The current system also appears to discourage welfare recipients
from returning to the job market. Expanding the number of people eligible for state help (say, through the gradual introduction
of a guaranteed annual income) and easing tax rates on the middle class would probably improve the distribution of income in
the province.[38]

The level at which taxes are administered can also affect the
efficiency of public investment and the timeliness of initiatives to
improve business conditions. Six metropolitan areas (Montreal,
Quebec City, Gatineau, Sherbrooke, Saguenay, and Trois-Rivières)
now account for 70 per cent of Quebec's population and jobs. Yet,
they lack the financial levers to match their growing responsibil-
ities. Decentralizing a share of the province's taxing authority to
them could result in better decision making and improved maintenance of major infrastructure.[39]

Promoting Enterprise. Another drawback is that, despite spectacular successes in some areas – like building subway cars for
New York City, managing airports in France, or developing the
triple drug therapy against HIV/AIDS[40] – Quebec has not been
successful in encouraging the emergence of entrepreneurs. While
the number of those wanting to set up a business has risen, the actual number of new Quebec enterprises has fallen sharply in the
last fifteen years. In 2015, only a third of business owners blamed
government regulation for this.[41] Cultural factors, including an
aversion to risk, the fear of failure, a lack of perseverance and
innovation, suspicion of wealth in a once highly Catholic society,
and high tax rates may be more important factors. One reason
that income distribution is better in Quebec than in Canada and

the United States may be that very few really rich people decide to live there permanently.

Other Measures. The economy can also be strengthened by reducing the role of monopolies, taking advantage of opportunities for free trade, fostering the expansion of Quebec's multinationals, making tax credits for research and development fairer and more efficient, improving health and social services, and continuing to overhaul the province's often decrepit infrastructure.[42]

The Limits of Ideology

This is a rich menu, with some measures likely to be more straightforward than others. There is also room for debate about the proper balance between promoting efficiency and safeguarding familiar programs. Open and informed discussion is needed to strike the right balance. And here is where Quebec runs into another challenge. More than in other parts of Canada, idealism can assume a particular edge there, souring into ideology. Sixty per cent of Quebeckers vote for centre or centre-right parties, and many conservatives vote *indépendantiste* because they regard achieving political sovereignty as more important than improving the economy. But a significant and vociferous minority, who regard themselves as "progressive," regard almost any government cost cutting or measures to encourage business as retrograde and even inhuman.

Yet, very few of the policy changes mentioned above lend themselves to cut-and-dried decisions. There is no left or right solution to improving the quality of investment in education or stemming high school dropout rates. Infrastructure policy is not so much about "whether or not" as about "how much" and "where." Even tax policy does not have to become a minefield if the constraints of the current system are properly identified, a large number of taxpayers benefit from the reforms, serious efforts are made to close loopholes and tax shelters, and there is no fraying of the social safety net for those who pay no taxes at all.

Consider two issues that illustrate the limits of ideology: university tuition fees and government support to business.

Tuition Fees. In early 2012, students across Quebec reacted angrily to the news that the government was to raise what were the lowest university tuition fees in Canada – and would remain the lowest, even after the increase. Gabriel Nadeau-Dubois, one of the leaders of what was to be known as the "'Maple Spring," ridiculed the government's claim that there was not enough money to keep tuition fees unchanged. There seemed to be funds, he said, to spend on bad management and advertising and new buildings and high salaries for university presidents and to give tax handouts to corporations. "Funny, isn't it? Apparently money is in short supply only when it's convenient for it to be in short supply. There is no lack of money in Quebec."[43]

But other voices expressed views that did not always chime with their usual ideological positions. The social democrat Jean-François Lisée (who was later elected leader of the main *indépendantiste* party, the Parti québécois) supported higher tuition fees as they would prevent a business owner with just a high school diploma from having to contribute to the education of the daughter of a couple of doctors.[44] Éric Duhaime, the dyspeptic conservative economist we met at the start of this chapter, might have argued that all students should borrow for their studies rather than depend on government. Instead, he suggested that baby boomers should pay higher fees for their health services before young people were asked to spend more for college, as they were already shouldering a higher share of their education costs than their parents had.

How government should promote higher education – through low-cost student loans (which might increase individual responsibility and performance) or keeping tuition fees low (which can complicate the financial planning of university administrations) or a mixture of the two – was a practical matter open to a range of opinions and concerns. Nonetheless, Nadeau-Dubois treated all opponents of the student strike as "neo-liberals" and labelled eminent Quebec economists as "bookkeepers" devoted to the idea of "every person for himself" that was slowly replacing the principles and institutions "that have forged the identity and soul of modern Quebec."[45]

Business Subsidies. Government support for the private sector also transcends standard ideology. Conservatives generally oppose direct government support for the private sector as an interference in the market, with the potential for creating favourites, bankrolling inefficiency, and wasting taxpayer money. Social democrats tend to be more sympathetic to identifying possible "winners" and risking public resources to create jobs and strengthen specific industries. They also expect the beneficiaries to be grateful for state help and behave accordingly. Yet, for decades, both sides have supported a large government role in Quebec industry as a means of promoting employment, deepening the province's expertise in some areas, and widening its markets.

In 2000, provincial and local governments in Quebec were already supporting business at the rate of $469 per person compared with an average of $193 in Canada and $32 in Ontario (in 1997 dollars).[46] The largest recipient was Bombardier, the aircraft manufacturer based in Montreal that has relied on government favours from 1986 onwards. Some analysts even doubt that Bombardier would have survived without taxpayer help.[47] True to form, in June 2016 the Quebec government announced that it would invest US$1 billion in the company to try to shore up prospects for a new jet that was proving expensive to build and difficult to sell. Shortly after, Quebec's Caisse de Dépôts said that it would purchase $1.5 billion of stocks in Bombardier's more dynamic and profitable railway subsidiary, bringing total new support to more than $2.5 billion.

Following these announcements, school teachers and police officers, whose own salaries and pensions were being curbed by a "lack of resources," were shocked and disgruntled. Shortly thereafter, the political class as a whole reacted angrily when Bombardier announced it would be outsourcing some of its production to India, Mexico, and Morocco. The mood soured further in March 2017 when the company awarded its six top executives a 50 per cent pay rise. This was deferred until 2020 after more public fury.[48] Then, in October 2017, to skirt punitive duties announced by the US government, Bombardier ceded a 50 per cent share of its new jet program to the European giant Airbus, which revealed that it would now locate final assembly of the airplane in the US state of Alabama. And in November 2018 Bombardier announced that it was eliminating twenty-five hundred jobs in Quebec.

Some would argue that, as one of Canada's largest exporters of manufactured products, responsible for sixty-five thousand direct and indirect jobs and accounting for up to a third of Quebec's foreign sales, Bombardier is a special case.[49] In their view, government should support its operations to the full extent compatible with international trade rules. But, for a number of very sound reasons, propping up private companies has opponents at both ends of the political spectrum.

I asked the "godfather" of state assistance to private enterprises, Bernard Landry, who pioneered such schemes as minister of economic development in the late 1970s and early 1980s, whether he thought the results had been up to expectations. He had no doubt about it, citing the example of the computer game, animation, and virtual reality industry of which Montreal is a world hub. But he recognized that, from the start, people had their doubts. When he announced to the cabinet that he was offering help to the fledgling Cirque du Soleil to acquire a run-down warehouse in the Old Port of Montreal, his colleagues were aghast: "What? You're lending money to a *circus*?!" Others still have their doubts. I asked one of Quebec's best-known economists, Pierre Fortin, what he thought. "Honestly," he told me, "I haven't done any sustained research on the subject. There have certainly been some spectacular failures. But, in general, it seems to me like a roll of the dice."[50]

However, there is not always a great deal of leeway in policymaking. In its early days, the Liberal government of 2014–18 gored a number of sacred cows, with impressive results in budget savings and reduced borrowing. Although it was anathema to nationalists, the government even considered doing away with collecting Quebec's own income taxes (the only province in Canada to do so), which might have saved about five hundred million dollars per year. But, after first cutting back subsidies to Montreal's computer animation industry, the government restored them to their original level, persuaded that they were crucial for protecting jobs and maintaining the "cluster" effects of having such businesses concentrated in the metropolis. These subsidies were so attractive that, in 2015, French film-makers produced the animated version of the iconic *Le Petit Prince* (The Little Prince) in Quebec. In September 2017, five former ministers of finance argued publicly that such support had made Montreal one of the world's top five cities in artificial intelligence, animation, visual effects, and computer games production.[51]

Resistance to Change

As these examples suggest, in economic and social policy there is legitimate room for debate and even second thoughts when experience and data are looked at properly. But, unfortunately, in Quebec name-calling often precedes such analysis. Part of this can be explained by the nature of the political system, which creates artificial enemies or under-represents important strands of opinion, magnifying differences and suspicions. Advocacy groups also sometimes take positions that are counter to the interests of society as a whole. To quote Claude Castonguay, one of the doyens of social policy in Quebec, "In the debate between the Minister of Health and the head of the medical specialists' union in 2012 about a possible pay increase for general practitioners, it was difficult to see which side was worrying about the patients and taxpayers. What is clear is that the sum total of the interests of pressure groups does not add up to the well-being of the public. Except in rare cases, consensus and compromise aim at keeping the peace rather than serving the public interest."[52]

Some resistance to change also stems from an understandable attachment to the "Quebec model," an approach to economic and social policy inspired by the European welfare state, which itself has been undergoing review and rebalancing even in its heartland, Scandinavia. Some aspects of the Quebec model have allowed the society to catch up with other economies. But other features have held it back. In the words of one disgruntled economist, "Groups who are poorly organized, like taxpayers and consumers, lose out to highly organized ones like trade unions which, despite their rhetoric, are conservative defenders of the status quo. Why is such 'corporatism' worse in Quebec than in other places? And why is competition seen as a zero-sum game, rather than as a way of increasing the size of the collective pie?"[53]

Claude Castonguay, who promoted the Quebec model actively as a politician and businessman, thinks it has now run its course. "It allowed us to become a relatively prosperous people in greater control of our destiny. But, with the passage of time, it has turned us into a society that is developing below its potential and is not completely aware of the situation it is in."[54] Others might argue that, tested rather than tattered, the Quebec model still means something and that it has allowed the society to weather the occasional economic storm without being thrown off course.

Part of the resistance to reform is also an expression of existential insecurity. Following the battle over tuition fees, the student leader Gabriel Nadeau-Dubois said that he opposed letting universities become "centres of excellence" closely linked to industry and the broader needs of the economy, as this would jeopardize public education and culture, particularly in an "uncompleted, culturally fragile land like Quebec."[55]

The residual influence of the Catholic Church is also strong, decades after most Quebeckers stopped going to church. Even staunch secularists can appear steeped in the church's social teaching. In the words of one recent writer, "Prisoners of a delirious greed and a false sense of freedom, individuals are now just wheels in a soulless war machine, pitting a small number against the human race as a whole. Yet, since Aristotle's time, we know that to live a full human life, we need the community. 'A stone,' to quote Antoine de Saint-Exupéry, 'has no hope of being anything but a stone. But, joining with others, it can become a temple.'"[56] These sentiments are attractive on their own terms but could be seen as paternalistic when applied to economic policy.

For fifty years, Quebec politicians have been building a mixed economy in the face of globalization and doing so with considerable success. It is thanks to good public policy that income distribution is better in Quebec and France and Germany than in the United States and that poverty is at its lowest level in decades. Respecting the mix of factors that keeps an economy lively is not a concession to "individualism" so much as a proper response to experience and public expectations of a better life. No prominent politician in Quebec wants to unleash the forces of an "unfettered" market. Most simply want to strike a balance between efficiency and fairness, after their own lights.

Pauline Marois, who was premier for eighteen months (2012–14) but originally a social worker associated throughout her career with a broad range of progressive causes, has expressed her frustration with the attitude of some Quebeckers: "Wealth creation is not an end in itself but THE essential condition for promoting equality of opportunity, funding public services and social programs, and building real solidarity. We cannot redistribute money that we don't have. We need to put an end, once and for all, to this fear of wealth as if it were something that turns us away from the common good. On the contrary, it's wealth that allows us to make common cause with those who are in need."[57]

Managing Quebec's Debt

Marois also knew that much of Quebec's progress was built on other people's money. Perhaps the nadir of the Quebec model was Premier Lucien Bouchard's secret visit to Wall Street in June 1996. (He even hired a private plane so as to keep it quiet.) Having heard that the bond-rating agency Standard & Poor's (S&P) was about to lower the province's credit rating yet again, thereby raising the cost of future borrowings, he decided to argue the case face to face. "It was like being in court," he recalled.

> I asked them to give us another chance, saying that we were putting our public finances in order. We had even reduced public sector salaries by six per cent the week before. They answered that Quebec had been going its own way for 40 years and the results were hardly brilliant. We had

been borrowing for years without really adding things up, so it was normal for them to be sceptical. I pleaded with them, as if it were the cause of my life. After three or four hours, they said they would call us the next day. Our credit rating remained intact but we were to be put under tighter surveillance.[58]

Thereafter, governments of every hue have made better debt management a cardinal principle of economic policy. Perhaps only people who have never paid a mortgage will be surprised by this. In 2006, Quebec created a Future Generations Fund into which a portion of budget surpluses was to be placed to cushion young people against the burden of future financial obligations they had no role in contracting. The government also committed itself to reducing the size of Quebec's debt to 45 per cent of GDP by March 2026. (It dropped from 61 per cent in 1995 to 50 per cent in 2009, then sprang back to 55 per cent in 2014.)[59] Progress since then has been so steady that in December 2018 Quebec's new government announced that the province would meet its planned debt ceiling by 2021, five years ahead of schedule.[60] S&P, the same bond-rating agency that berated Premier Lucien Bouchard twenty years before, upgraded Quebec's debt in June 2017 (from A+ to AA-), surpassing Ontario's credit rating for the first time.[61] And in July 2018, Quebec was borrowing money at lower interest rates than any other Canadian province except British Columbia.[62]

Economic performance has improved so much that young people now appear to be better off in Quebec than in Ontario. Youth unemployment is lower and those without jobs usually find one faster. Young Quebeckers work shorter hours, yet have higher median incomes and purchasing power. Like all comparisons, this one is subject to caveats. Ontario suffered more from the 2007–8 financial crisis and later from a strong Canadian dollar, so the last ten years have not been its best. Quebeckers also benefit from two special factors: subsidized daycare (which saves them more than a thousand dollars per child per month) and low housing costs (which are not usually the sign of a dynamic economy).[63] Partly as a result, the size of Quebec's middle class has remained generally stable, while that class has been shrinking in some other societies.[64] Tides will turn. Quebec's per capita income ($46,000 in 2015) is still lower than Ontario's and Canada's ($55,000).[65] And social and economic policy must continue to keep pace with new developments, with efficiency and a strong social safety net in mind. But, for now, Quebeckers are much better off than many of them realize.

Ten years ago, a study by the Quebec Ministry of Finance established that if the province were a country, it would be the twenty-sixth richest in the world (based on GDP figures adjusted for purchasing power). But it would lag behind Canada, the United States, and most European countries, including small ones like Ireland and the Netherlands. Compared with other Canadian provinces and US states, Quebec would rank much worse: fifty-fifth out of sixty, with only New Brunswick, Nova Scotia, Prince Edward Island, Mississippi, and West Virginia trailing behind it. Yet, argued Alain Dubuc, columnist with Montreal's *La Presse*, Quebec should be able to do better. It was the only urbanized and industrialized economy at the bottom of the chart, with a network of universities and excellent cultural facilities. "How is it," Dubuc asked, "that a people wanting to assert itself doesn't do all in its power to excel economically, where the crux of the battle lies? Quebec's problem is not that it lacks ideas. It lacks courage. And I'm not talking about politicians, who simply reflect the society that elects them. I'm talking about collective courage."[66]

Quebec's economy is much stronger than it was ten years ago, but Dubuc's challenge still rings true. And – as we have seen – new challenges abound. One is a fast-aging population. An even greater one is global warming.

5

Climate

If Quebec has distinguished itself by asserting its identity and strengthening its social democracy, it has also led the way on climate change. In 2006, Quebec was the first government in North America to set emission reduction targets under the 1997 Kyoto Protocol. They were also the most ambitious. The following year, Quebec was the first jurisdiction on the continent to introduce a carbon tax. In 2008, it joined the Western Climate Initiative, a group of US states and Canadian provinces committed to introducing a "cap-and-trade" system.* Quebec was also the first government outside the United States to adopt California's tough automobile emission standards. Since then, it has pressed successfully for provinces, states, and regions to be given official status at international gatherings on climate change alongside national governments.[1]

---

* Cap-and-trade systems allow companies to buy and exchange emission rights while committing themselves to steadily reducing their generation of greenhouse gases. Governments establish an absolute limit on emissions, adjust these downwards periodically, and sell rights within that ceiling that can be exchanged in the market. Companies that no longer need those rights (because they have met their reduction targets) can sell them to others who need more time to adapt. Governments typically devote the resulting revenues to green investments, like public transport or municipal energy efficiency programs, although in British Columbia the revenues are distributed to the general public. In 2013–20, Quebec expects to raise $3.3 billion through such trades.

One of the world's most successful international environmental treaties has been headquartered in Quebec. The Montreal Protocol, approved by UN member states in 1987 and monitored in Quebec's metropolis, has eliminated 98 per cent of the gases that caused the opening of the "ozone hole" over Antarctica. The hole has been shrinking and is expected to close completely in twenty to thirty years.[2] Combatting climate change will be more complicated than fixing the ozone hole, but this experience will prove valuable.

Has Quebec's leadership on climate change been reflected in practical efforts to do something about it? Before answering that question, we need to look at the issue from a global perspective.

The Global Challenge

Scientists have been studying climate change since the late nineteenth century, and the debate about it has been intense for so long that it is easy to forget that, as a subject of government policy, it is only thirty years old. Canada played a central role, hosting the first international scientific conference on the subject in Toronto in June 1988,* as well as an important UN meeting in Montreal in 2005 that finalized the details of the 1997 Kyoto Protocol. Since then, Canada has made history in a different way, being the first and only country to withdraw from the Kyoto agreement to escape hefty fines for failing to meet emission reduction targets. Despite the disappointment of climate-change activists, that decision made some sense because of Canada's size, harsh winter, and exports of oil and gas that make the challenge of adjustment far greater than for smaller, more densely populated nations like France and the United Kingdom. Undoubtedly, Canada could have set more realistic targets and tried to adhere to them

---

* Entitled "Changing Atmosphere – Issues of Global Security," it was co-chaired by Norwegian prime minister Gro Harlem Brundtland and Canadian prime minister Brian Mulroney on 27–30 June 1988.

more rigorously, but to many it seemed deeply unfair to punish Canada when much larger emitters of greenhouse gases (Brazil, China, India, and the United States) were exempt from binding targets.

Given the scale of the challenge, the subject can breed a sense of helplessness and fatalism, with the result that concrete progress is often overlooked. In March 2015, the International Energy Agency (IEA) announced that global emissions of carbon dioxide had stabilized in 2014. This was only the fourth time in forty years that this had happened, and on the three previous occasions it was due to sudden slowdowns in the world economy: the oil shock and US recession of the early 1980s, the collapse of the Soviet Union, and the 2009 financial crisis. This was the first time since 1974 that emissions had levelled off in conditions of general economic improvement in the world.

Surprisingly, China – the world's biggest carbon polluter – was largely responsible, by using steadily less coal since the 1980s and sharply increasing its recourse to hydroelectric, wind, and solar power.[3] Overall electricity consumption in China is also growing more slowly as the government imposes energy efficiency standards on industry, shuts old factories, and shifts away from heavy manufacturing.

Rich countries are also playing their part. In the five years preceding the IEA report, their economies grew by nearly 7 per cent but their emissions dropped by 4 per cent.[4] Owing to the sharp fall in the use of coal for power generation, the United Kingdom has reduced its total carbon emissions to their lowest level since the 1920s.[5] Sweden has committed to being carbon-free by 2045.[6] Quebec has made progress, too, reducing emissions by 8 per cent between 1990 and 2013, while the population grew by 17 per cent and GDP by 56 per cent, representing a drop of almost 22 per cent per Quebecker.[7] However, global progress has now stalled. After three years in which global emissions levelled off, they started to rise again, and by the end of 2018 – apparently because of prolonged low oil prices – emissions were accelerating, in the words of one scientific study, "like a speeding freight train."[8] But our ability to bring them under control has been demonstrated.

What the World Can Do

Climate change is complex, and economists were woefully slow to take it into account, but conventional economic policy can still help to fight it. The IMF estimates that removing subsidies for petroleum products, electricity, natural gas, and coal could lead to a 13 per cent decline in carbon dioxide emissions. Such a measure would of course require a large number of people to heat their homes and cook differently. More research and development on renewable energy would also help as R&D spending is typically a tiny fraction of the amounts spent on energy subsidies.*[9]

Another encouraging fact is that green investments will eventually pay for themselves through lower operating costs and reduced damage to the atmosphere. Nor will they require steep increases in government revenues to pay for them. The World Bank estimates that by 2030 annual investments of up to $1.1 trillion will be needed to reduce carbon emissions to an acceptable level.† More ambitious targets would raise the bill to $1.7 trillion. Yet, governments could save as much as $1.2 trillion simply by eliminating subsidies on energy, agriculture, water, and fisheries, all of which encourage excessive use of scarce natural resources. Not all of this will be freed up to fund green investments, as some governments will want to protect subsidies for the very poor, while targeting them more effectively. But a large part of these savings could be used to make growth less wasteful and dirty.[10]

Lifestyle choices can also help. According to a study conducted by Dalhousie University, if meat consumption in rich countries dropped from ninety to fifty-three kilograms per person per year, global emissions from agriculture would fall by 44 per cent. A British study found that if the wealthy in the world confined themselves to four small portions of meat and a quart of milk per week, agriculture's contribution to global warming would be cut

---

* In 2010, R&D on clean energy amounted to $9 billion compared with $480 billion spent on subsidizing traditional fuels.
† "Acceptable" means to maintain a 50 per cent chance of not exceeding global warming of 2 degrees centigrade above pre-industrial temperatures by 2100.

to zero.[11] And meat-eaters abstaining from beef have a carbon footprint only ten per cent higher than vegetarians.[12]

Citizen activism is important, too. In just ten years (2007–17), a campaign spearheaded by the Sierra Club – combined with a drop in the price of natural gas – contributed to halting the construction of 120 new coal-fired power plants in the United States (out of 150 originally planned) and hastened the phase-out or closure of 240 others, accounting for one-third of installed capacity.[13]

Some observers complain that rich countries bear too much of the burden of fighting climate change and point out that developing countries have put as much CO_2 into the atmosphere in the last fifty years as advanced ones have done in two and a half centuries.[14] But, given their head start in using up the world's resources and their privileged access to the necessary knowledge and technology, it is not unreasonable to expect wealthy nations to take the lead. In two and a half days, an average American pumps as much greenhouse gas into the atmosphere as a Tanzanian does in an entire year.[15] Rich countries also have a special opportunity to promote changes in consumption and production that boost demand for green technologies, stimulate innovation, and allow a scale of production that will lower the cost of those technologies. Germany's aggressive policy on promoting solar power was critical to boosting global demand for solar panels, thereby reducing their cost.[16] As a result, in 2014 Bangladesh already had three million home solar systems, second only to Germany.[17]

But the global challenge remains colossal. More than 1.2 billion people in the world still do not have access to electricity, and countries like India (already the third-largest emitter after China and the United States) are thinking of building highly polluting coal-fired plants, locking in the risk of rising emissions for decades. As CO_2 lasts so long, global emissions (currently thirty-seven billion tons per year) must eventually be lowered dramatically rather than just brought under control. Fortunately, technical progress is accelerating. In 2015, the International Energy Agency estimated that renewables like wind and solar already account for more than half of total global growth in electrical generation. The cost of solar energy has dropped so sharply that India could provide solar lanterns to the seventy-five million households lacking electricity simply by redirecting three years of subsidies on kerosene.[18] And India has already committed itself to producing almost 60 per cent of its power from green sources by 2027.[19] Indeed, for China and India, pervasive urban smog has turned a long-term challenge into an immediate political priority.

Green growth will require changes in pricing, taxes, regulation, and public investment, as well as intelligent programs of public awareness that explain the long-term benefits of changing our habits now. The subject is volatile, as no amount of improved efficiency and new technology is likely to preserve the current consumption patterns of middle-class people in rich and poor countries. But the consequences of inertia will be even more explosive.

A sense of wonder at the beauty and fragility of the Earth, a deep appreciation of its gifts, an honest appeal to our consciences, and a sense of solidarity with the rest of humanity will be critical to finding the right answers. And sitting on the fence is not really an option. In the words of Wendell Berry, one of the great prophets of the conservationist movement in the United States: "We must understand that fossil fuel energy must be replaced, not just by 'clean' energy, but also by *less* energy. The unlimited use of *any* energy would be as destructive as unlimited economic growth or any other unlimited force. If we had a limitless supply of free, non-polluting energy we would use the world up even faster than we are using it up now. If we are not in favour of limiting the use of energy, starting with our own use of it, we are not serious."[20]

Good public policy, international cooperation, and an intelligent use of markets can all help achieve a better balance of growth and stewardship of the world's resources. But – as Berry suggests – it will also require moral choices. Gilles Brien, a Quebec meteorologist at Environment Canada for thirty-three years, echoes that view. "We have no choice but to act. Even if it is a little late to stop climate change, it is not too late to moderate or adapt to it. And we shouldn't rely entirely on new technology. All that does is persuade us that we don't need to change our habits, which is where we should be concentrating our efforts."[21]

What Quebec Is Doing

Now, let's return to Quebec. Although Canada's per capita emissions (twenty-four tons) are among the highest in the world, Quebec's are the lowest in the country (ten tons).[22] That is due less to enlightened policy and individual or collective efforts than to the fact that Quebec has 40 per cent of Canada's water resources and that 90 per cent of its power is hydroelectric, with the rest coming mostly from wind. In fact, 99 per cent of the energy it produces is renewable, making it almost unique in the world.[23] That the province is not a significant oil and gas producer is also important. But other facts are less encouraging.

While transportation accounts for 17 per cent of global emissions, its impact in Quebec is more than twice as large (38 per cent) and even higher in Montreal (58 per cent). Yet, major infrastructure investments in recent years were expected to increase the number of cars entering the city by about one hundred thousand a day. In fact, Quebec spends 70 per cent of its transport budget on roads and 30 per cent on public transport, exactly the opposite of what Ontario does.[24] In Montreal, there has not been a single extra Métro station or other major mass transit investment in twenty-five years.[25] The initial cost of one road project, the Turcot Exchange in Montreal ($1.5 billion) was thirty times higher than the government budget for promoting cleaner transport.[26] Partly as a result, overall progress is disappointing. While industry reduced emissions by 20 per cent between 1990 and 2012, transport went in the opposite direction (increasing them by 26 per cent).[27] One reason is that the number of private cars went up three times faster than the population.[28] At current rates, the province will meet barely a third of its 2030 emissions target.*

This is hardly surprising, given the lack of a serious climate-change culture in the province. Public service announcements or publicity campaigns on the subject are rare, despite

---

* In September 2017, the Ministry of Finance estimated that emissions in 2030 would be only 14 per cent below the 1990 level compared with the target of reducing them by 37.5 per cent.

the long-standing commitment of the government to fighting climate change and its willingness in other ways to reach deep into people's lives. In November 2015, Quebec's new tobacco law was hailed as the most progressive in the world, banning smoking at playgrounds and sports fields used by children, requiring a minimum size for cigarette packages (to ensure that warning labels were readable), outlawing flavoured cigarettes popular with young smokers, imposing the same restrictions on electronic cigarettes, and making it illegal to smoke in a car with someone under sixteen. The law passed the National Assembly unanimously.[29]

Local governments, too, are capable of stern measures. In February 2016, councillors in the Montreal borough of Verdun decided to ban new drive-through windows at restaurants and businesses to cut down on emissions from idling cars and encourage more physical exercise. (Quite naturally, the Tim Hortons national coffee chain fought back, as half of its revenues came from drive-through windows.)[30] But province-wide programs aimed at major causes of emissions and toxic waste (like non-biodegradable plastics) or promoting improved agricultural and land-use practices are lacking.

Like many people elsewhere, most Quebeckers seem to regard lower emissions as desirable rather than vital. Nowhere is that nonchalance more evident than on the road. Many Quebec drivers are aggressive and discourteous and unlikely to respect speed limits for any reason, let alone environmental ones. In the words of Jacques Gérin, a former federal deputy minister for the environment, "Once the average Quebecker – or average Canadian for that matter – has sorted out his rubbish and put it in the bin of the proper colour, he feels he has done most of what he needs to do to save the planet."[31]

Canada produces 2 per cent of the world's total emissions with less than one-half of one per cent of global population, making it the highest emitter per capita after Australia and the United States.[32] But that fact is little known and certainly not widely propagated. In Quebec, green activism has been focussed on blocking new oil pipelines, opposing oil and gas exploration, and promoting more bicycle paths. The nitty-gritty task of tackling known sources of carbon emissions has not been central to the debate.

Furthermore, rhetoric and decision making do not always match. At the UN Climate Change Conference in Paris in December 2015, Quebec's premier told a press conference that the province was a global leader on the subject and that "all the world is talking about us." Then, he was forced to defend the government's decision to allow oil and gas exploration on Anticosti Island and construction of a $1.1 billion cement plant in the Gaspé region without a review by the province's environmental impact assessment agency. (The plant was expected to create four hundred jobs but also to become Quebec's number one industrial gas polluter.)[33]

Construction and waste management practices also need to be kept under tight review, as buildings account for about 40 per cent of all energy consumption in the world and as much as 75 per cent of carbon emissions.[34] In this respect, cities need to take the lead. Former New York City mayor Michael Bloomberg argues that cities are the key to saving the planet even if their very existence sometimes seems contrary to nature. "Why? Because most urban residents live in apartments that are smaller than the average American home and require far less energy to heat in winter and cool in summer. City residents also tend to drive less, because they can walk, bike, and take mass transit to get around. As a result, the average per capita carbon footprint in New York City is two-thirds smaller than the national average."[35] Quebec's metropolitan areas (Montreal, Quebec City, Gatineau, Sherbrooke, Saguenay, and Trois-Rivières) are not as dense as Manhattan, but account for 70 per cent of the population and can hence organize efforts to slow climate change more effectively than small towns.

Fortunately, government is acting decisively in some areas rather than waiting for public awareness to prompt it into action. The tough automobile emission standards introduced in 2016 were approved with the support of all four political parties in the National Assembly. By 2025, almost a quarter of all vehicles sold in Quebec will need to be electric or hybrids. To prepare for this demand, charging stations are being installed all over the province as part of the first public network of its kind in Canada. Already, Quebec has almost half of all registered electric cars in the country.[36] The government is also investing more in public transport, although the largest project announced to date, an electric rail line linking the centre of Montreal with the western suburbs, has been criticized for favouring richer neighbourhoods at the expense of the city's less affluent East End.[37]

In other respects, too, the seeds of change appear to have been sown. Attitudes to new forms of energy are remarkably positive, despite the low cost of hydroelectricity. Studies suggest that southern Quebec could produce as much power from wind as the entire province does from water. Local residents can overcome reservations about windmill installations quite quickly, if they are properly involved in the planning. And it is no longer an axiom that new energy capacity should be hydroelectric, given the environmental damage caused by dam construction.[38]

More Needs to Be Done

Overall, however, Quebec seems to underestimate the size of the challenge it faces, caused in part by setting targets over relatively short periods. The real challenge is not to cut emissions by 37.5 per cent between now and 2030 but, rather, to reduce them by 80 per cent by 2050, the next milestone set by the world's scientific community. That will mean eliminating them by 100 per cent in most respects, as all industrial and agricultural practices cannot be expected to change without imposing a heavy price on living standards. Short-termism may also result in wasteful expenditure, such as conversion from oil to natural gas only to have to replace natural gas facilities in the next stage of adaptation. It would be better to make a clean break from past practices wherever possible than to build up to them slowly.[39]

Quebec is doing better than all other provinces (except Newfoundland, PEI, and Nova Scotia) in reducing emissions, but the next stage will be much more difficult. In just seven years

(1979–86), by electrifying home heating and a broad range of industrial activities in response to high international oil prices and the coming on stream of major new hydro capacity, the province accomplished four times more than it did in twenty-three subsequent years (1990–2013). The targets Quebec has set for itself remain highly ambitious and the path to reaching them has not been mapped. The biggest challenge will be in road transport, with heavy trucks accounting for a third of total emissions in the province and smaller vehicles (cars, SUVs, light vans) responsible for just under a quarter of the total.[40]

The province has experience and expertise to build upon but does not always marshal them effectively. Following the flooding of the Saguenay River in 1997 and the crippling ice storm of 1998, Quebec set up a unit to predict the effects of climate change and help the provincial and municipal governments and key actors like Hydro-Québec better plan their decision making, including their choice of infrastructure. That climate-modelling capacity now allows the province to predict rising water levels and other effects of climate change, placing it in the international vanguard of adaptation in the field. Unfortunately, the unit has not been given the resources or authority to apply its models to the planning of emission reductions as well.[41]

Quebec has also re-established an agency to promote energy efficiency, called Transition énergétique Québec, but critics complain that it has not been given the power to intervene directly in the full range of greenhouse-emission issues. Nor have key ministries like Environment, Transport, or Municipal Affairs been asked to cede any budget or powers to the agency. According to Normand Mousseau, professor of physics at the Université de Montréal and one of the most informed and compelling voices on climate change in Quebec, "This refusal to act decisively to move government policy in a coherent direction is based partly on the myth that we have already mastered the energy transition and that we can continue to operate as we have always done while protecting the 'Quebec model.'"[42]

Steven Guilbeault, another prominent actor in the climate debate, agrees that Quebec has a long way to go to live up to its commitments. A one-time Greenpeace activist and co-founder of the advocacy group Équiterre, he was arrested four times for disturbing the peace, including scaling the CN Tower in Toronto in 2001 to promote the Kyoto Protocol. Later, he headed the Montreal Chamber of Commerce's committee on sustainable development and a Quebec government team studying the potential for new forms of energy in the province. A believer in positive reinforcement, he insists that Quebec can still be a trailblazer, like Sweden and California. "We have the know-how, the tools, and the resources. All we need to do is use them."[43]

It is possible that the October 2018 election will prove a turning point in public and political attitudes to climate change in Quebec. For the first time, the subject was debated openly during the campaign, and the incoming premier admitted that perhaps he had treated the subject too lightly in the past. Within weeks of the election, fifty thousand people marched in Montreal to promote Le Pacte pour la transition (The pact for the [energy] transition), an impassioned appeal by leading Quebec ecologists, artists, and writers to do more to reduce emissions. But early signs suggested that the new government would find it as difficult as any other – in the words of French president Emmanuel Macron – to reconcile worries about the end of the world with many people's concerns about the end of the month.[44] Two weeks after the election, the new conservative cabinet was split down the middle about whether to approve a fertilizer plant that would create two hundred jobs but emit as much CO_2 as 180,000 extra automobiles on the road. The "economic" ministers won the day.[45]

6

Fairness

So far, we have looked at how Quebec's identity, sense of community, economic and social policy, and concern about climate have distinguished it from other societies. I have described Quebec as it *is* rather than as it *should be*, and I have kept personal views to a minimum. Now, I want to change course to a degree. In this chapter, I will examine two important reforms – a guaranteed annual income and proportional representation – that I believe are essential for making Quebec an even healthier society. They are also consistent with the level-headed and even-handed approach that the society has taken in other respects. In these areas, personal and political judgments are as important as the facts; so, I will present the case for and against such reforms as objectively as possible, before expressing my own view. In the next and final chapter, I will offer personal conclusions on the broader range of issues covered in this book.

In November 2006, in an effort to recycle some of its excessive profits, the Quebec liquor monopoly (SAQ) offered scratch coupons at the counter for discounts of five, ten, and fifteen per cent. In one store, a customer asked for a second coupon when she drew the lowest number. The cashier refused. "But you don't know who I am!" she retorted, identifying herself as the interim head of the SAQ and insisting vehemently that she be treated differently. "I don't care who you are," the employee answered. "It's against the rules." In due course, it was the boss, not the cashier, who lost her job.[1] In other countries, the outcome might have been different. But in Quebec, a central part of the cultural heritage is a British sense of fair play. That inheritance could be built upon in two important ways: in reimagining the social safety net and in ensuring that every person's vote is worth the same.

A Guaranteed Annual Income

I suggested in chapter 3 that a guaranteed annual income might be a way of reconciling greater efficiency in the use of public funds and greater simplicity, security, and dignity for those in need. The idea is not new. In his *Utopia* (1516), Thomas More (1487–1535) suggested that it was better "to provide everyone with some means of livelihood, so that no one is under the frightful necessity of becoming a thief, and then a corpse [i.e., being hanged]."[2] The American rebel Thomas Paine (1737–1809) designed the first detailed scheme but restricted it to a one-time "endowment" payment at the age of twenty-one and an annual allowance to everyone over fifty. The great liberal writer John Stuart Mill (1806–73) sounded quite Marxist in seeing a guaranteed income as an apparent answer to the "social problem of the future," which was "how to unite the greatest individual liberty of action, with a common ownership of the raw materials of the globe, and an equal participation of all in the benefits of combined labour."[3]

More surprisingly, two highly conservative economists who taught at the University of Chicago in the second half of the twentieth century, Milton Friedman (1912–2006) and Friedrich Hayek (1899–1992), espoused a "negative income tax" that would top up the incomes of anyone earning less than a specific amount. Hayek admitted that there were difficult questions about determining the precise standard of living to be protected, "but there can be no doubt that some minimum of food, shelter and clothing, sufficient to preserve health and the capacity to work, can be assured to everybody." While highly suspicious of state intervention in general, Hayek insisted that government should provide "outside the market a uniform minimum income for all those who for some reason are unable to earn at least that much in the market."[4]

And, in his last book, Martin Luther King Jr. (1929–68) argued forcefully for a guaranteed income: "The dignity of the individual will flourish when the decisions concerning his life are in his own hands, when he has the assurance that his income is stable and certain, and when he knows that he has the means to seek self-improvement."[5]

Support for the idea across the political spectrum has emboldened its proponents and created what some describe as an international "movement." In Canada, its best-known champion is the former Conservative senator Hugh Segal, who has been pressing for it for over a quarter of a century: "We don't have to accept a hodgepodge of programs. Welfare doesn't support anyone – it ensnares and entangles. It creates judgment. It is deeply problematic, wasteful, and expensive. The idea [of basic income] is attractive for all. Just give the money to the people living in poverty who will know what to do with it."[6] Segal points to the 1975 introduction of a guaranteed annual supplement for seniors in Ontario that was later turned into a federal program. "Seniors were buying cat and dog food to augment their diets. [Afterwards], poverty went from 35 percent of this population to three percent."[7]

In its purest form, a guaranteed or basic income would be paid to everyone, rich or poor, whether they were working or not, and recovered at higher income levels through the income tax. The big difference for the poor is that any extra income earned on their own would not be taxed at 100 per cent or cause them to lose their eligibility (as under many current welfare programs). It would also be paid monthly. Hence, they would have an incentive to increase their earnings rather than be caught in a low-income "trap." The universality of the program would remove the stigma associated with social assistance while the lack of conditions (such as a willingness to seek work) would lessen the cost of administering the program.

Some proponents rhapsodize about the idea. "It is an essential element of a radical alternative to both old socialism and neoliberalism, of a realistic utopia that offers far more than the defence of past achievements or resistance to the dictates of the global market," writes Philippe van Parijs, a Belgian professor of economic and social ethics and author of the most comprehensive recent study on the subject. "It is a crucial part of the sort of vision needed to turn threats into opportunities, resignation into resolution, anguish into hope."[8] That "vision" sees a guaranteed annual income as a preparation for the day when automation and artificial intelligence will permanently reduce the number of jobs available, even to highly trained people, distributing social wealth as equitably as possible. Others see it as an answer to more pressing objectives, like providing more security to the poor, overcoming perverse incentives that can penalize work, and cutting back on unnecessary paperwork.

But even the most vocal supporters admit that there are potential drawbacks. One obvious objection is that some people would use an unconditional annual income not to look for a more satisfying or better-paid job or to improve their skills, but to stay at home and enjoy a "free ride" at the expense of the rest of society. That risk can be contained if the guaranteed income is modest. The concern of the Nobel Prize–winning economist Edmund Phelps (who once supported the idea) is that "all too many young people would lack the vision and will to resist yet another year of avoiding life's challenges and risks."[9] His preference is to raise wages through government subsidies to employers, but that would only help those currently working.

Until recently, the only notable Canadian experiment was in the town of Dauphin, Manitoba, in 1974–8. The most cited outcome was that only a small number of people stopped working, and they were principally mothers who stayed home and spent more time with their children. Some young people chose to remain in school longer. Visits to emergency rooms and recorded domestic abuse also dropped.[10] Other supposedly encouraging examples (from Namibia, Malawi, and India) are too outlandish to apply to Canada. In March 2016, with the help of Hugh Segal, the Government of Ontario announced a "basic income" pilot project in six selected communities that "could provide a new approach to reducing poverty in a sustainable way." For three years, beginning in November 2017, the experiment was to track whether the program not only met basic needs but also improved participants' diets, mental health, use of medical services, housing, and access to education and training. The impact on employment and participation in the labour market was also to be measured.[11] However, in August 2018 the new (conservative) government of Ontario decided to cancel the study.[12]

The trouble with experiments is that they are short lived. People will react differently to a guaranteed income over two or three years than they might if they knew it was for life. Some of the problems it is meant to solve (like persistent high levels of unemployment in Europe) do not exist in Quebec, and others (like increasing the bargaining power of workers vis-à-vis their employers or paying women for household work) would not strike many taxpayers as high priorities yet. Unless a basic income paid for itself by replacing existing social programs, it could be seen as another burden on public finances just as Quebec is emerging from decades of debt and high taxes. Nor would it be responsible to propose an ambitious new social program too lightly, given the need expressed earlier in this book for a better balance between economic efficiency and social justice.

Yet, given Quebec's leadership on social policy and its success in fighting poverty to date, testing a more radical approach to income support seems a coherent next step. Many Quebeckers would sympathize with the views of the Norwegian social philosopher Jon Elster, who notes that the state of the social sciences is "light-years away" from allowing us to predict the long-term effects of major social changes of this kind and that "society cannot underwrite the pet ideas of each and every enthusiast who offers a panacea for our problems." But he concedes: "Very little would be lost by implementing the proposal on a small scale, by a low-level guaranteed income. If it turns out that it has the predicted effect, one could then increase the guaranteed income up to the point, if any, where further increases begin to have adverse effects."[13]

A basic income policy would establish an income floor just above the poverty line that would ensure that all Canadians met their basic needs. In 2013, the Fraser Institute calculated that Canada's current income support system (payments plus administration) costs $185 billion. According to one estimate, a guaranteed annual income ($20,000 per adult, $6,000 per child) would cost $40 billion. One can also assume major savings in health costs as a result of better nutrition and housing.[14] But this is only an approximation. Conservative think tanks often overstate the size of government while social advocates will tend to underestimate the true costs of major initiatives. What is certain is that a full-blown guaranteed annual income for everyone would be extremely expensive.

Of course, there should also be savings. A basic income would not replace essential social programs like family and child care, mental health and addiction services, and social housing. Nor need it do away with disability assistance or unemployment insurance. But, at a minimum, it could replace existing income-support programs like welfare, Old Age Security, the GST rebate, the Canada Child Tax Benefit, and many other tax credits. And a guaranteed annual income would deal directly with poverty rather than through programs that are not always well targeted or are highly indirect like minimum-wage legislation.[15]

More than a hundred mayors across Canada have endorsed the idea of a basic income. This is significant, as it can be argued that they are closer to the reality of poverty than other politicians. Calgary mayor Naheed Nenshi notes that it would be the equivalent of an extension of the Child Tax Credit "except that it would be for all Canadians who might drop below the poverty line."[16] Denis Lapointe, the mayor of Salaberry-de-Valleyfield, a town of forty thousand on Montreal's South Shore, believes that a guaranteed annual income would allow twenty-two- to twenty-three-year-old high school dropouts stuck in low-paying jobs to begin taking adult education classes and improve their skills.[17]

An August 2018 poll showed that about 60 per cent of Canadians support the introduction of a guaranteed annual income, and almost certainly the number of Quebeckers who believe in it is even higher.[18] Yet, the committee set up to study the matter in Quebec recommended against it in November 2017 and proposed minor

improvements to existing welfare programs instead. Their reasons? Computer simulations suggested that those who were "least
needy" might benefit the most from the program and that the government would not be able to afford it.[19] Opposition politicians and
poverty groups criticized the committee's lack of "ambition," and I
agree with them. Simulations are notoriously unreliable in predict-
ing the dynamic effects of major policy reforms, and the least Quebec can do is to follow Ontario's example, organize a pilot project,
and (unlike Ontario) go through with it. It is quite possible that a
guaranteed income will seem commonplace in Western countries
twenty years from now, but to date no country has actually adopted one, and it is only appropriate that Quebec should prepare
the ground carefully.

The Case for Proportional Representation

The second respect in which Quebec's sense of fairness could be
reflected more faithfully in its national life is electoral reform.
Proportional representation could lessen political posturing and
bickering and give citizens a sense that their vote really counted.
This would also encourage them to participate in elections more
often or at least to do so with greater thoughtfulness, conviction,
and satisfaction.

Canada's voting system has worked well for most of our history but, beginning in January 2006, when the Conservative Party
governed for nearly a decade with only 36–39 per cent of the vote,
many Canadians have begun to question the merits of the Westminster "first past the post" system. The May 2015 election for
"The Mother of All Parliaments" was a sterling example of how
the model can fail. The British Conservative Party won a resound-
ing majority with only 36.9 per cent of the vote (331 seats). The
right-wing United Kingdom Independence Party (UKIP) won
12.6 per cent support (a third of the Tory vote) but only one seat.

Many Canadians might vote "no" to the question: "Should experts be asked to alter our democracy in a way that has never
been tried before in North America?" But Quebeckers would

probably be more forthcoming, if asked: "Should your party receive the same proportion of seats in the National Assembly as its total share of the vote?"

One common argument against proportional representation is that it can encourage a splintering of parties and lead to frequent coalitions, raising the spectre of instability, like Italy's sixty-two governments between 1945 and 2008.[20] Forming coalitions can prove messy – as in Belgium (2010–11), Spain (2015–16), and Germany (2017–18) recently. But they generally work well in Europe, reflect public opinion and diverse interests more accurately, and – in the eyes of reformers – constitute a more modern and reliable way of determining national policy. According to *The Economist*, thirteen of the world's fifteen top-ranked democracies use proportional representation.[21] Nor are coalitions – formal or informal ones – unknown in the British system. Canada was created by a coalition government (1864–67) and had another during the First World War (1917–20). More recently, the United Kingdom ran a stable multiparty administration between 2010 and 2015.

A second disadvantage is that proportional representation can sever the personal connection between politicians and their voters, because one method of topping up the seats of smaller parties is to draw candidates from a reserve list attached to no specific constituency. But, like now, voters would still have someone to approach with a problem, even if they did not vote for the person directly. Besides, de-linking votes and geography seems a minor concession to make, compared with asking Québec solidaire voters to accept that in the 2014 election only a third of their ballots counted.*

A final concern about such a reform is that fringe parties can have an outsized say in the forming of governments and force coalitions in directions that do not reflect mainstream opinion. But it is also true that treating small parties seriously and giving them a seat at the table can moderate their views. Some electoral systems exclude minor parties altogether, but doing this

---

* In the 2014–18 National Assembly, a proportional system would have given Québec solidaire nine instead of three members.

can appear arbitrary and water down the benefits of proportional representation. Germany, for example, requires that parties receive five per cent of the vote before qualifying for seats in the Bundestag. Partly as a result, Angela Merkel came close to winning a majority in the 2013 election with only 42 per cent of the vote.

In the 2014 Quebec election, if all votes had been treated equally, the Liberal Party would have fallen short of a majority and entered into a coalition with the Coalition Avenir Québec. In October 2018, the CAQ won a majority of seats with only 37 per cent of the vote. Under proportional represenation, the party would have continued in an imaginary coalition with the Liberals but taken over the premiership and received a larger number of Cabinet positions.

Between 2003 and 2007, five provinces (including Quebec) studied the options for changing the voting system, and all five concluded that proportional representation was desirable. But weak political leadership (including a "hands-off" approach by the five premiers) and poor public information stopped these proposals in their tracks.[22] Three provinces (British Columbia, Ontario, and Prince Edward Island) held referendums, and only in BC in 2005 did more than half of the voters support the idea.* BC held another referendum on the subject in November-December 2018, with 61.3 per cent voting "no."

A system of proportional representation would not only be fairer to voters and keep false "majorities" out of power. It could also tone down unnecessary passion and pettiness in Quebec politics. According to Colin M. Macleod, professor of law at the University of Victoria, "the fact that advancing a legislative agenda depends crucially on cooperation with one's political opponents provides an incentive for civility and mutual respect." At election time, it would also be harder to denounce former allies if a coalition had produced respectable results.[23]

---

* Even then, the proposal did not pass, as BC set a double threshold for approval: an overall vote of 60 per cent and a simple majority in 60 per cent of the districts.

Quebec's political parties have studied electoral reform repeatedly but not pursued it very hard until recently. Senior *indépendantiste* politicians, including the former premier Bernard Landry, have told me that they have always supported the idea but did not want to implement it until the Parti québécois had actually won more than half of the popular vote. (They never have.) Failing that, the current system worked in their favour. Unlike other Canadians, Quebeckers were largely sympathetic to forming a coalition government at the federal level in 2008, but that idea was scotched when Prime Minister Harper prorogued Parliament to escape a vote of non-confidence and the Liberal Party changed its leader.

Interest in the subject peaked again during the 2015 federal election, when many Quebeckers were forced to vote "strategically" rather than for their preferred party to avoid dividing the progressive vote and allowing the Conservatives to squeeze back into office. The Liberal leader Justin Trudeau vowed that it would be the last election fought under the old rules, but he changed course two years later, apparently recognizing that his party would lose seats under the new system. The leader of the Green Party, Elizabeth May, described this as a "betrayal" – particularly of young people eager for a different style of politics – while the NDP considered it "one of the most cynical displays of self-serving politics."[24] The following week, Quebec's three Opposition parties pressed the government to introduce electoral reform at the provincial level, albeit with a technical twist to protect the interests of the "regions" (i.e., rural voters). The government responded that the current system served Quebeckers well.[25] In May 2018, all three Opposition parties committed to introducing electoral reform if they formed the next government, and in November 2018 two former heads of Elections Quebec and Elections Canada called for a change in the system.[26]

Such facts suggest that, if a referendum were held in Quebec, proportional representation would probably be approved. But, given the failure of such exercises elsewhere in Canada and the particularly painful history of referendums in Quebec (none has been held on any subject since 1995), it would appear more appropriate to appeal to the traditional solidarity of the political elite to introduce it after an appropriate round of public explanation and consultation.

In any event, given the potential for backsliding on the subject, even when avowed supporters of proportional representation have formed a government, continued public pressure will be needed to force the remaining sceptics among Quebec politicians to recognize that this is an issue of reason and fairness.

7

Looking Ahead

"The most difficult thing for a politician," René Lévesque once said, "is to retain one's ideals while losing all one's illusions."[1] So, too, for a society. Thirty years after he died, how might Lévesque have answered the two sets of questions posed at the beginning of this book?

Identity. How can the *Québécois* be reassured that their culture and language will be properly protected? Or should they accept that past efforts in that direction have been largely successful and see Quebec's situation in a more positive light? How can this identity be reconciled with a more diverse society?

Economy. Given Quebec's high levels of debt and taxation, how can it maintain an acceptable level of social services without continuing to shift the cost to future generations? And how can Quebec become more efficient, not just in the traditional economic sense, but also in fighting poverty and climate change?

Let's start with identity.

Quebec nationalism has always been of a rather mild variety. Three days after 9/11, I attended a concert at the Kennedy Center for the Performing Arts in Washington, DC, and was surprised by the sight of the Stars and Stripes hanging over the stage and the playing of the national anthem. It was an all-Beethoven program, including the Ninth Symphony and its famous ode to international fraternity, making the symbolism all the more jarring. That was the reaction of an international civil servant but also of a Canadian who had always thought of patriotism as functional rather than visceral, as a convenient glue for keeping the pieces of the mosaic together. Unlike American or French "exceptionalists" or even some Canadians who now compare themselves with others, Quebeckers have never boasted about being better than anyone else. They may have been haughty at times towards the million French speakers elsewhere in Canada apparently buckling under Anglo-Saxon pressure, but that reflected Quebec's own nervousness rather than any sense of triumphalism. As nationalists, all that Quebeckers have ever wanted was to be able to live in their own tongue.

The last fifty years have transformed Quebec in many ways, but its essential values – including some Catholic ones – remain largely intact. Quebec was "distinct" well before there was a constitutional debate about how to deal with that fact. In an 1898 national referendum, every other Canadian province voted to ban the production and sale of alcohol; but 81 per cent of Quebeckers said no.[2] During two world wars, the province opposed military conscription not just firmly but vociferously. For twelve years (1976–88), the province ignored federal law on abortions and refused to prosecute cases until Ottawa caught up with them and legalized the procedure. More recently, opinion moved heavily against the conflict in Afghanistan even as other Canadians were still wrapping yellow ribbons around trees to honour the troops. And in 2008, when three federal parties proposed to pull the plug on a minority Conservative administration and form a coalition government, most Quebeckers backed the idea while the rest of Canada regarded it as foul play.

The values that unite Quebeckers – their *joie de vivre*, common sense, courtesy, concern for the downtrodden, aversion to conflict, and refusal to be homogenized by globalization – are more important than anything that divides them and, ironically, make Quebeckers the most "Canadian" of all Canadians. Those values helped them weather important storms in the past and will prove vital in meeting future challenges.

The greatest of those challenges remains the cultural one. There is a special pleasure – but also a special responsibility and burden – in being French. The American novelist Henry James (1843–1916) wrote that "what happens to France happens to all that part of ourselves which we are most proud of, and most finely advised to enlarge and cultivate and consecrate ... to make the earth a friendlier, an easier, and especially a more various sojourn."[3] The English invented steam power and the spinning jenny, which set off the Industrial Revolution and transformed our ability to create lasting wealth. They also gave the world a galaxy of literary and artistic geniuses, including the greatest of all writers. But France has offered us a parade of smaller Shakespeares and, along with the Italians, the refinements of fashion, art, cuisine, conversation, debate, and intellectual exploration that have enriched us in a deeper sense.

Sometimes, like fighting climate change, defending French culture can seem like a hopeless cause. In September 1938, less than two years before German troops overran France, the French writer Georges Bernanos reflected: "Somewhere in the world, as I write this, a young Frenchman is asking himself: 'Is it worth saving my country? For what purpose?' I have always asked the same question, and it is because I pose it that I am French. When I stop asking it, I will be dead and deserve my rest. There is no pride in being French, just a great deal of effort and work."[4]

A Solid Foundation

To their everlasting credit, Quebec nationalists – whether federalists or *indépendantistes* – have achieved what many of them may have doubted would be possible at the start. They have established a sound foundation for securing the future of the French language. Parts of the process were painful, and the diehards were often unduly belligerent towards others. But without their passion and stubbornness, who can say how far Quebec would have come?

Despite the violence of the late 1960s, that process has been remarkably peaceful. Indeed, compared with truly complex, multi-ethnic societies like Russia, India, and Indonesia, Canada and Quebec have had an easy time of it. On 1 October 2017, hundreds of Catalans were reportedly injured by Spanish police as they tried to vote in a referendum on independence and, the same day in Cameroon, seventeen members of the English-speaking minority were killed while protesting against discrimination. (That is more than all of Quebec's political fatalities since the 1837–8 Rebellion.) But serious damage was done all the same, and many are still nursing their wounds.

Between 1972 and 2013, 1,033,402 people left Quebec to live in Ontario – most of them during the mid-1970s and mid-1990s – dividing families, interrupting or ending careers, and creating bitter memories.[5] Thousands more moved to other provinces. Entire groups, including much of the South Asian community, shifted from Montreal to Toronto. Unlike most other provinces, Quebec still loses about 100,000 residents per year (net migration is about 13,000), which suggests that, for many, the drawbacks of living there outweigh the attractions.[6] Ontario has also been losing people, apparently for economic reasons, but that is more recent, compared to an established pattern in Quebec. Such numbers suggest that issues of identity and economic opportunity continue to weigh on those who are young, talented, ambitious, and hence mobile – the very people who should be at the heart of what the French call the *forces vives* (the vital forces) of a society.

The restlessness at the heart of Quebec society – with almost one in two French speakers still hoping for their own country – will not dissipate quickly. But as some hopes dim, bright realities take their place. Many young Quebeckers have only a faint idea of the strife that made it possible, but they see French as a birthright rather than something that they need to fight for. And, in Montreal, they shift from speaking French to speaking English with a self-confidence that borders on insouciance in the eyes of those who bear the scars of earlier battles.

Continuing Debate

In the meantime, nationalists do not need lectures from outside, as their own debates are already lively enough. Some deride the unflappability of their fellow citizens, their aversion to politics, and their lack of assertiveness. But their patience, understanding, and prudence have proved valuable. The *Québécois* may have overcome a sense of insignificance (*petitesse collective*), their deference to the church, and a tendency to fall back upon themselves (*repli sur soi*). But the marrow in their bones – their realism and long-suffering – has not changed very much. René Lévesque linked Quebec's identity to its wish to survive. To be *Québécois*, he thought, "means above all else that we are attached to this sole corner of the earth where we can be fully ourselves." "We are heirs," he added, "of the fantastic adventure of an America that once was almost entirely French, and of the collective stubbornness that permitted this living part of it – Quebec – to endure. This is the basis of our personality. Those who don't feel it, at least occasionally, are not one of us."[7] That last sentence may appear a little sour now – and potentially divisive. But it reflects the long-standing worry of a nation that knows it must adapt to changing times – and immigration – while protecting the bonds that keep Quebec intact.

The philosopher Charles Taylor has pointed out that past debates about identity were contemptuous and polemical, with antagonists trying to discredit each other as petty and intolerant. "But definitions of identity develop out of our deep experience, and for that reason they deserve a degree of respect, even when we think they are mistaken."[8] According to the historian Jocelyn Létourneau, for many *Québécois* the "English" were the ones who prevented them from realizing their full potential, while for many "English," the *Québécois* are a bunch of childish complainers who need to accept that they were beaten in 1759 and move on to other subjects. History teachers, Létourneau thinks, should challenge these tidy versions of events and make young people comfortable with ambiguity and paradox.[9] "You must be conscious of where you come from in order to avoid disappearing into the reel of human destiny. At the same time, it would be wrong to think that remembering the past is only liberating. When it leads to ancestors dominating the world of the living, it can obscure the self."[10]

One of the most balanced commentators on Quebec's existential worries is Daniel Jacques, a philosophy teacher at

François-Xavier-Garneau College in Quebec City and author of *La Fatigue politique du Canada français* (The political fatigue of French Canada). He is chillingly clinical about revered historical figures, seeing René Lévesque as part of a long line of "beaten heroes" running from Montcalm (the vanquished general of 1759) through Papineau (the leader of the 1837–8 Rebellion). He thinks Lévesque should have resigned on the night of the 1980 referendum rather than prolong people's hopes of a better outcome the next time around. "Instead, he opened up another chapter of the endless ambivalence and uncertainty in our history."[11] Professor Jacques believes that the Parti québécois should abandon the idea of independence and focus on the protection and development of Quebec culture. "Like individuals, entire peoples sometimes have dreams that inspire them to live for a while beyond their usual possibilities. Such dreams can also collapse into bad faith and denial and a diminishment of oneself. The boundary between the two is not easy to define and sometimes we go through a great deal of hardship before waking up from unhappy dreams."[12]

Although he still believes that an independent Quebec would have been better for everyone, he thinks Quebeckers should now abandon the *best* and accept what is just *better* for the society. "Yes, we can wait patiently for Canada as a whole to trip up in another round of constitutional negotiations which could lead to a revival of interest in sovereignty. But that is highly improbable and an accumulation of small missteps would hardly qualify as a glorious new beginning for the people of Quebec." The *Québécois*, he thinks, should become French Canadians again, accompanying other Canadians in a common adventure of "building a more just democratic society in this part of North America." "This would allow us to look ourselves in the eye more serenely and fairly. We would need to accept that our status as a national minority was permanent but celebrate the numerous successes of contemporary Quebec."[13]

Not all *souverainistes* feel defeated. "Certainly, young people are not supporting the cause any longer. But why should that surprise anyone?" asks Gérard Bouchard, the sociologist and brother of a former premier. "They are in a globalized world where it is harder to find one's bearings and the more adventurous among them have opportunities that didn't exist for our generation. Instead of trying to make them feel guilty, we should be happy that they are capable of expressing themselves and succeeding in the face of worldwide competition and we should adopt them as models. The cause of Quebec independence is still too steeped in the values and experience of those who founded it. We need to reinvent it."[14]

The long-time *La Presse* columnist Alain Dubuc takes up that theme differently. "Sovereignists have to find a new battleground for three reasons: for their own mental health (in their position, I would be exhausted); because endless dissatisfaction leads nowhere and makes day-to-day life less bearable; and because stirring up issues of language and identity plays into the hands of the most intolerant members of society. A dynamic economy, an explosive cultural life, and exemplary talent would give Quebec the protection it needs. Success on every front is the strongest and most persuasive form of national self-expression."[15]

Strengthening the French Language

So, what can others do to support those still fiercely attached to the future of the French language? First, they can use it as often as possible in public places and try to improve their knowledge of it continuously. There is no constitutional solution for discourtesy. Except for the very old – and even then – there is no reason why every Quebecker should not speak a reasonable amount of French. (In fact, the number who don't – about 5.5 per cent – is very small.)[16] For many Quebeckers, nationalist concerns compete with bread-and-butter issues. Defenders of the language must seek allies in more moderate tones and, occasionally, light-heartedly, celebrating the value of diversity in Quebec but also the rich gift of a French culture that continues to challenge, charm, and astound people around the world. It is no accident that France is still the most visited country on earth.

Quebeckers must also do more to celebrate and protect the French language not from external threats but from internal corruption. Some of the greatest critics of Quebec French are people who hardly know a word of it. To begin with, there is no such thing as a Quebec "accent." Instead, there are as many accents in Quebec as there are in France, the United States, and the United Kingdom. Besides, many educated *Québécois* take pains to use their language with a precision and elegance that would put some of their French cousins to shame. On top of that, Quebec has done more than France itself to keep their language contemporary while shielding it from the lazy adoption of foreign terms. A French culture minister in the 1980s named Toubon tried emulating Quebec's example but was ridiculed in the press as "Minister All Good" (a play on his name). Nonetheless, more needs to be done to strengthen the French language in Quebec. While much of the battle has been conducted on the high ground, fending off swarms of anglicisms as ferocious as hornets, the engagement has been virtually lost on the valley floor where English and *Québécois* syntaxes have largely merged.

The journalist and novelist Denise Bombardier is so confident of her own culture that she lambastes both the Mother Country and narrow-minded zealots back home, without stopping to catch her breath. Her *Open Letter to the French, Who Think They Are the Navel of the World* (published in 2000) sold more than 250,000 copies, most of them in France. At home, she is almost vitriolic in opposing the "Creole-ing" of Quebec and those who think that preserving the national slang (*joual*) is key to remaining *Québécois*. She sees this as "cultural regression" and "clannishness," shutting the place off from the wider world.[17] There is a link, she thinks, between the deterioration of Quebec French and the fading interest in promoting it. "We have lost respect for our language. Otherwise, we would speak it with more pride and real fear about using it badly. People who speak their language properly are not usually asked where they come from." Many immigrants, she says, know that some spoken French in Quebec is poor and learn it only reluctantly. "In the history of Quebec, there has always been a large number of people who, through laziness, lethargy, fatigue, or mere acceptance of globalization, want to play down the 'old' approach to language. Well, unless we treat the language as somehow sacred, French will not resist the forces of Anglicization."[18]

Quebec should also consider a suggestion made more than ten years ago by Jean-François Lisée, who was elected head of the Parti québécois in 2016, to merge the French- and English-speaking junior colleges (cégeps) into one bilingual system. This would prepare new generations to use both languages confidently and take advantage of the special opportunities bilingualism provides. Lisée insisted that second-language teaching in Quebec's high schools would have to be upgraded significantly to make such a measure possible.[19] Just as military conscription in Western countries once had the felicitous side-effect of strengthening national integration, bilingual colleges could do the same by exposing students to contemporaries from a wider variety of backgrounds.*

If people deserve to be addressed in their own tongue, so do English speakers, wherever possible. This is common courtesy and faithful to Jocelyn Létourneau's elegant notion that Quebec is a society of "double inspiration." Most Quebeckers appear to recognize that mutual respect is contagious, even if some politicians benefit from division. The motion passed in the National Assembly in November 2017 to discourage shopkeepers from greeting customers with the phrase "Bonjour/Hi" is a good example of theatrics trying to triumph over good instincts and manners.

Only a small number of nationalists are bitter and vindictive. Others are beginning to recognize that developments are moving in their favour. About three-quarters of Quebeckers are expected still to be speaking French in 2050, and half of the world's seven thousand languages will survive for another fifty years after that. French will be one of them. Particularly important for Quebec is that over thirty years (1971–2011) the proportion of immigrants able to converse in French doubled (from 40 per cent to 80 per cent) while 42 per cent are at least trilingual.[20]

---

* In a 17 September 2018 televised election debate, Lisée distanced himself from this proposal, knowing it would be controversial with English-speaking voters.

Building on Diversity

While making common cause in defending the French language, Quebeckers can also recognize the advantage of speaking English. The year that Jean-François Lisée wrote his essay *Nous* (2007), Quebec was already exporting half of its products to the rest of North America and three hundred of its enterprises were employing sixty thousand Americans. "Hence," Lisée wrote, "English will remain an indispensable part of the Quebec economy and it would be a fantasy to want to impose French as the 'only language' in all [export] businesses." The ability of Quebec scientists and researchers to collaborate with colleagues in Europe and the United States also allows it to learn from some of the most innovative societies on earth, making it, in Lisée's phrase, a potential "bridge" between two worlds. "While remaining economically competitive, Quebec has no other choice but to set itself apart, build on its difference, and even shout it out, so as to become even more interesting, welcoming, and dynamic tomorrow. In a new century, where innovation is the key word, originality is the path to success."[21]

If the foundations of its identity remain strong, Quebec needs to handle supposed threats to it with greater aplomb. One of the most touching things I heard from young *indépendantistes* was their answer to my question: "What is the unique 'brick' that an independent Quebec would bring to the construction of a better world that it cannot do as part of Canada?" In different words, their answer was the same: the promotion of cultural diversity. In two important ways, in its treatment of English speakers and its attitudes to Islam, Quebec is failing in that respect.

Although Quebeckers are generally happy, with 75 per cent of French speakers believing that they are living in a "just society," only 40 per cent of English speakers feel the same.[22] In late 2017, Montreal's two major French-language dailies published cultural highlights for the autumn without mentioning a single English-language play, and the Théâtre du Nouveau Monde produced a Bertolt Brecht play with eighteen actors all of whom were white. In contrast, an English-language company named Teesri Duniya (Hindi for "Third World") had mounted plays for more than thirty-five years that, according to a prominent figure in English theatre, reflected the people on the street and the Montreal Métro and "the real new world of Quebec." The Théâtre du Nouveau Monde received $1.5 million a year from the government, while Teesri Duniya had been told that they would no longer be getting support.

"What must we do," asked Guy Sprung, "to be accepted as Québécois? In a society where minorities are tragically killed in their places of worship [a reference to the shooting of six people at a Quebec City mosque in January 2017], is it not possible that theatre could play a rather important role in bridging Quebec's solitudes?"[23] For the most part, English Quebeckers have been remarkably patient in recent years, recognizing the long-simmering frustrations that the *Québécois* suffered for decades. But it would be ill-advised to take such patience for granted. Deep down, many English speakers harbour emotions that can turn ugly. The most dramatic example of that was the attempted assassination of the newly elected *indépendantiste* premier Pauline Marois at her victory rally in downtown Montreal on 4 September 2012 by a man screaming, "The English are waking up."

Discomfort with Islam

Islam is the second respect in which the province must come to its senses. In August 2016, a number of Quebeckers took up the issue of the "burkini" – the full-length bathing suits that some women were wearing on French beaches. They were not very different from the ones that French women favoured at the beginning of the twentieth century and are now charmingly depicted in popular postcards at French coastal resorts. All the same, some mayors were suggesting that such bathing suits be banned. The Quebec minister for women's affairs responded, quite sensibly, that that controversy should be allowed to fester on the other side of the Atlantic. Only those who have an almost religious belief in *laïcité* will see a religious "statement" in a Muslim woman trying to cover herself up on a beach.

Not every accommodation to other people's religions can be described as reasonable. Muslim women cannot expect the health service to have a woman doctor available at all times to look after them, any more than they should object to unveiling themselves for a reasonable identity check. But judging others on the basis of their religion contravenes the sense of common decency of which Quebeckers are justly proud. Nor should they see the Muslim veil as a provocation any more than Jews, Muslims, or atheists should regard the crucifix above the Speaker's Chair at the National Assembly as an act of proselytism. It is a reflection of the province's history and traditions. Even secular Muslim women who oppose the wearing of headscarves warn against forcing those who do so to stay indoors.

More broadly, a large number of Quebeckers are now Muslim. That fact is irreversible. Montrealers – who are most exposed to such diversity – are generally comfortable with it. The rest of Quebec should catch up with them. Politicians, too, should stop using religion to divide Quebeckers. During the 2016 Parti québécois leadership campaign, Jean-François Lisée criticized a rival for sending greetings to constituents on the occasion of Muslim feasts. When it was pointed out that Lisée regularly wished people "Merry Christmas" and "Happy Easter," he replied lamely that they were no longer regarded as religious occasions.[24]

The killing of six people at the Grand Mosque in Quebec City in January 2017 was not an isolated act. It was the culmination of a series of hateful incidents in the previous months, including a xenophobic debate about the installation of a Muslim cemetery in a small town near Quebec, the sending of an offensive package to the Grand Mosque, the burning of the car belonging to the chairman of the mosque's board, and acts of vandalism against Muslim sites across the province. Salt was added to those sores in the following months by an acrimonious debate over whether to set up a commission to study systemic racism, the revival of tensions about Muslim clothing when the National Assembly returned to the issue of secularism in late 2017, a sometimes-insensitive debate about how to commemorate the January killings, and disagreement on whether to institute a national day of opposition to Islamophobia.

In the words of Imam Hassan Guillet, writing in La Presse in January 2018, "Quebeckers are far from being racists, xenophobes, or anti-Muslim. The very presence of so many new

Quebeckers like myself is proof of how open, generous, and welcoming this society is. But we have to be honest with ourselves and stop hiding behind the killer and saying it was the act of a single man. An atmosphere already existed that led directly or indirectly to the act."[25] On the day after the killings, thousands of people across the province attended night-time rallies to show their solidarity with the families touched by the violence. But at the one I attended in downtown Montreal, while most people were solemn and quiet, a sizeable number were smoking and cracking jokes as they waited for the speakers to take the stage. That nonchalance suggested a mechanical and sentimental reaction to events rather than a real awareness of the dangers ahead. The fight against Islamophobia must be just as intense as that against anti-Semitism, reflecting not only the basic decency of most Quebeckers but also the positive value of *laïcité* as a shield for believers and non-believers alike against bigots of all kinds.

When he retired from politics in October 2018, the outgoing premier Philippe Couillard spoke for many in calling for "an inclusive society where everyone is invited to the table. A place where people are judged by what is in their heads, rather than on them. For what they have in their hearts. For what they have to offer to the rest of us."[26]

Now, let's turn to the economy and the social safety net.

Economic Reform

At the moment, Quebec is enjoying a remarkable combination of growth, employment, and reduction in poverty. No one can predict how long this will last. The fact that rich countries are in a "sweet spot" of low interest rates and low oil prices probably has as much to do with it as effective policymaking. But this situation will not endure, and governments and entrepreneurs must be able to react quickly to new circumstances. Nor is there room for self-satisfaction. Unemployment in the Montreal region has never been so low since Statistics Canada first started collecting regional data, but the city still ranks at the bottom of the fifteen largest cities in Canada and the United States in per capita income.[27]

Institutional changes could help guide policy adjustments. An independent budget review office at the National Assembly (like those in Washington, Ottawa, and London) would add realism and honesty to debates about government accounts. Independently funded bodies for highway and school maintenance could also cure major weaknesses in infrastructure and the quality of schooling. But changes in public attitudes will also be necessary to release pent-up energy and innovation in Quebec.

The first of those attitudes concerns the role of the state. Simon Langlois, a professor of sociology at Laval University, suggests that on "moral" subjects like euthanasia, gun control, norms for criminal sentencing, and the legalization of marijuana, Quebeckers are well to the left of the rest of Canada. But attitudes to the economic role of the state are edging closer to the re-evaluation underway in the rest of the country.

For fifty years, the *Québécois* were keen supporters of government intervention, as it allowed them to gain economic ground and was closely tied to affirming their national identity. To this day, they remain proud of such institutions as the Caisse de Dépôts, Hydro-Québec, and the Société d'assurance automobile Québec (SAAQ).* But people are now more divided about how much longer Quebec can afford its programs of income redistribution and collective financing. The debate about university tuition fees and the trimming back of once-generous pension schemes for civil servants are two examples. The perceived sacrifices necessary to fight climate change may also fuel differences.[28] It is perhaps no accident that the proportion of the population now supporting centre and centre-right parties (60 per cent) is the same as the number of people paying taxes.

I believe that Quebeckers must change their outlook in two important ways. First, while there has been progress in the right direction – people under thirty-five are now even more ambitious than other Canadians[29] – many of their elders must still

---

* The Caisse manages $250 billion of funds for Quebec's public pension and insurance schemes, while the SAAQ is responsible for all car-related matters, including registration, safety, and public no-fault third-party insurance.

overcome their Catholic suspicion of business and success. To repeat Pauline Marois's words, "We need to put an end, once and for all, to this fear of wealth as if it were something that turns us away from the common good. On the contrary, it's wealth that allows us to make common cause with those who are in need."[30] Second, "progressives" – those, like me, who feel that society is only as well off as its most vulnerable members – should stop automatically questioning efforts to manage public funds prudently. Or they should suggest constructive alternatives rather than disparage the motives of those in office. Trimming government programs that are out of date or can be delivered more cheaply is not a raid on the resources of the poor. On the contrary, it can free up funds for social programs. Similarly, there is no ideological answer to the aging of the population, only an array of unpleasant options. Very few really rich people live in Quebec, and there are reasons for that. Here are some of them.

Although Bombardier and the cluster of companies specializing in computer games and virtual reality in Montreal have been generously supported by government, not all enterprises have the space and backing they need to adapt to changes in the market. Nor have past subsidies improved overall productivity very much. The Montreal business school HEC (Hautes Études Commerciales) suggests that a better strategy might be to focus on innovative small and medium-scale enterprises or to lower the tax burden on Quebec companies, which is 30 per cent higher than in Ontario.[31] Bureaucracy can also be stifling. According to Pierre Goulet, who ran a successful printing company in Montreal, the fiscal incentives for small businesses can seem attractive at first but are so complex and numerous as to resemble a labyrinth "where a mother would lose her kids even in the company of a guide."[32]

Until recently, investors have also been constrained by a shortage of venture capital and by income tax rates that seem to punish success. Most economists agree that Quebec's tax system should be modified to better reward personal effort, investment, and savings. Tax relief in 2017–18 was welcomed by the middle class but denounced by the Opposition as "electioneering" and by advocates for the poor as funded by cutbacks in social programs. The latter claim is hollow. The 40 per cent of Quebeckers who pay no income tax have little personal stake in public policy and only a limited basis for challenging the trade-offs that governments must make between efficiency and welfare. And the 60 per cent who do pay taxes have every right to insist on better management of their dollars.[33] Taxpayers are also entitled to draw a distinction between labour "rights" and union privileges and to demand changes to restrictive practices that add to the cost of public programs. Organizations that serve the poor should see these reforms not as an assault on the disadvantaged but as a continued effort to protect the integrity of social programs through the elimination of waste and inefficiency in all aspects of government spending.

Although I treated it separately for ease of presentation, fighting climate change should be regarded as an integral part of economic policy rather than as a parallel set of concerns. Quebec's future choices and technological and commercial success will depend on how successfully it embraces the challenge. Although its heart is in the right place, its head is still distracted, and more must be done to mobilize public support and focus laser-like on the right priorities. The place to begin is reducing emissions in the transport sector.

Strengthening the Social Safety Net

Creating breathing space for entrepreneurs and investors and fighting climate change do not mean putting social protection at risk. The most important component of the safety net is the health system, where major reforms introduced in 2015–16 have yet to show reliable results. Waiting times in emergency wards have dropped by three hours since 2014 and now average 13.7 hours – still short of the undemanding target of 12 hours.[34] However, it will be some time before the wider impact of the recent reforms on health outcomes and government spending can be fairly evaluated. Some have denounced the approach as too highly centralized, even "Stalinist," but there is little doubt that drastic action needed to be taken.[35] In 2011, the Conference Board of Canada predicted that if nothing was done to stem the trend, health spending would go from about 50 per cent to 75 per cent of the province's total budget by 2030, threatening – in one commentator's words – the very survival of the Quebec state.[36]

But costs are only part of the challenge. Successive surveys have shown that Quebec has one of the worst-performing health systems in the country, and 79 per cent of Quebeckers say that their principal worry is about overcrowded emergency wards.[37] That is almost scandalous in the only social democracy in North America. If health services do not improve, Quebec should show some humility and consult other provinces about how they manage to deliver better results. And, if necessary, as a group they should challenge the 1984 Canada Health Act, de-emphasize hospital care, and introduce a greater role for the private sector. No other reform is as important for translating Quebec's renowned solidarity into concrete results.

Once again, like the Scandinavians, "progressives" must be open to fresh solutions. Norway and Sweden have private and public hospitals, decentralized systems (with regions and towns responsible for delivering care), and modest fees for doctor visits (that are waived for the poor).[38] Recognizing the limits of ideology in solving practical problems and tempering political rhetoric does not mean abandoning one's principles. Quebec has achieved a great deal through a mixture of passion and common sense and can continue to lead the way in North America in its efforts to balance efficiency and social justice. Introducing proportional representation and testing a guaranteed annual income would be true to that tradition.

An Unfinished Poem

Like any society, Quebec has its quirks. The *Québécois* have a strange and sometimes unpalatable sense of humour. They can also be infuriatingly patient in the face of provocation. But – except when they are behind the wheel – they are one of the most civil peoples on earth. And, despite their cultural insecurity,

Quebeckers are generally happy. More than 70 per cent of Quebeckers are satisfied with their lives, and older people are even more upbeat (81 per cent).[39] Nine in ten believe that society should ensure that people's basic needs are met. But a similar number think that differences in earnings are justified if they reflect individual ability.[40]

That sense of balance is a solid foundation for moving into unknown waters. Despite the hundreds of thousands of people who would still vote "Yes" in a referendum on independence, there are not all that many tortured souls in Quebec. No *indépendantiste* is waiting for permission to feel sovereign, and many Quebeckers already live in an "independent" state. Like British Columbians who do not really care about life in Manitoba or New Brunswick or about what is happening in Ottawa, people in Canada's second largest province feel generally self-sufficient. Crossing the border into Ontario, you don't need to be a sovereignist to feel that you are entering a foreign place, and few Canadians arriving in Quebec do not feel slightly disoriented. Some, like American tourists, go there for that very reason. And Quebec is not the only province that is proud of itself. One book about that seemingly plainest of places starts: "Saskatchewan is a state of mind."[41]

For Claude Castonguay, "Safeguarding our language will be an unending struggle whether we do it inside or outside Canada ... But most of it will depend on our vitality and attractiveness as a nation. We should get over our sense of fear, insecurity, and distrust. We have achieved enough in a number of areas to rival the best in the world. And as a people we have an important asset: that strong sense of solidarity that unites all Quebeckers."[42]

There will always be people who think of Quebec as an unfinished poem, and no one should begrudge them that. But beyond issues of culture and identity, Quebec, like Canada and other countries, faces serious economic challenges and strains on its democracy. As it overcomes its historical insecurity, it will enjoy advantages that many other societies would envy. And if "the past is prologue," Quebec's common sense, generosity, and persistence should steer it in the right direction – ensuring that it remains one of the most open and remarkable societies on earth.

Key Dates

1534   Jacques Cartier "discovers" Canada.

1608   Samuel de Champlain founds Quebec City.

1759   James Wolfe defeats French forces on the Plains of Abraham.

1760   *La Nouvelle France* capitulates to the British.

1763   The Treaty of Paris confirms British control over Canada (France chooses to keep Guadeloupe).

1837–8   Hundreds of French Canadians (known as *Les Patriotes*) rebel against British rule.

1867   Canada East (Quebec), Canada West (Ontario), Nova Scotia, and New Brunswick join to form a new country.

1898   In an early sign that Quebec is "distinct," every other province votes to ban the production and sale of alcohol; 81 per cent of Quebeckers say no.

1917   Quebec's premier Lomer Gouin allows a debate on whether the province should secede if the federal government insists on military conscription.

1927   French appears on Canada's postage stamps for the first time (sixty years after Confederation).

1960–6   The "Quiet Revolution." A highly reformist Liberal government accelerates social changes already underway.

1963   The FLQ (Front de libération du Québec) plants its first bomb in Montreal (20 April).

1970 The October Crisis. The FLQ kidnaps a British diplomat and murders the deputy premier, Pierre Laporte. The federal government sends tanks and troops into the streets of Montreal. Five hundred activists and intellectuals are detained.

1976 The Parti québécois wins power for the first time (15 November).

1980 First referendum on independence (20 May). Sixty per cent say "No."

1995 Second referendum (30 October). *Indépendantistes* lose by a narrow margin: 54,288 votes

Suggestions for the Future

Identity and Diversity

- Do more to use, celebrate, and protect the French language.
- Address English speakers in their own language, wherever possible ("Bonjour/hi" is perfectly all right).
- Get used to Muslim headscarves. Instead of thinking that women have been "forced" to wear them, consider other reasons they may be doing so, including natural modesty, a sense of style, and sheer convenience.
- Consider merging the French- and English-language junior college (cégep) systems into one to promote the better use of both languages and a deeper understanding between the two cultures.
- Think of Quebec as a society of "double inspiration," continuously enriched by other cultures as well.
- Take a cue from Quebec's highly successful artists, writers, film directors, singers, performers, and business people (i.e., be more self-confident).

Economy and Climate

- Organize a sustained public mobilization campaign worthy of Quebec's ambitious climate change objectives.

- Strive for green growth (i.e., promoting innovation and investment in energy conservation and other environmentally friendly industries). Move from words to action.
- Reform the tax system to reflect best practices in other rich countries with strong safety nets.
- Devolve more revenue-raising powers to Quebec's six largest cities (Montreal, Quebec City, Gatineau, Sherbrooke, Saguenay, and Trois-Rivières).
- Cut spending on new highways and increase investment in public transport.
- Reform the construction industry (i.e., do away with outdated work practices that add unnecessarily to costs while ensuring the continued protection of workers).
- Think hard about the continued need for generous subsidies to private businesses.
- Promote entrepreneurship and think positively about wealth creation.
- Stop thinking of government reform initiatives as a way of "getting at the poor." Regard them instead as a way of protecting popular social programs in the long term.
- Establish an independent budget review office at the National Assembly.
- Consider setting up independently funded bodies for highway and school maintenance.

Fairness and Solidarity

- Experiment with a guaranteed annual income, as a means of streamlining social spending and respecting the dignity of the poor.
- Introduce proportional representation, which would ensure that every political party obtained the same proportion of seats in the National Assembly as its share of the overall vote.
- Challenge the Canada Health Act to promote preventive care, de-emphasize the role of hospitals, and permit a larger role

for the private sector (as in France, the United Kingdom, and Scandinavia).
- Evaluate the performance of individual hospitals as a means of promoting efficiency and spreading best practices.
- Recognize the limits of ideology in solving practical problems.

Notes

Introduction

1 Louis Hémon, *Maria Chapdelaine* (London: Macmillan, 1923), pp. 195–6.

2 Willa Cather, *Shadows on the Rock* (1931), pp. 171–2.

3 Bruce Hutchison, *The Unknown Country: Canada and Her People* (Toronto: Oxford University Press, 1942), pp. 13–14, 36–8.

4 Paul-André Linteau, *Histoire du Québec contemporain*, Vol. 1; *De la Confédération à la crise (1867–1929)* (Montreal: Boréal, 1989), p. 69.

5 Graham Fraser, *Sorry, I Don't Speak French: Confronting the Canadian Crisis That Won't Go Away* (Toronto: Douglas Gibson, 2007), p. 105.

6 *Chicago Tribune*, 18 May 1963, pp. 1–2.

7 *Montreal Gazette*, 7 February 2017.

8 Maclure, *Quebec Identity*, p. xi

9 David Smith, conversation with author, 26 January 2016.

10 A November 2016 Léger Internet poll of 999 respondents showed 35 per cent of Quebeckers generally and 45 per cent of French speakers specifically supporting independence. (See *Montreal Gazette*, 19 November 2016, p. A14.) A May 2018 Ipsos poll showed a slight softening of support, with 31 per cent saying they would vote "Yes" in a referendum. Those votes were spread among three parties, the Parti québécois (68 per cent of whose voters supported sovereignty), Québec solidaire (41 per cent), and the Coalition Avenir Québec (25 per cent). See full coverage in *La Presse*, 3 May 2018.

11 Réal Menard, at the time a Bloc québécois MP in Ottawa and later mayor of Mercier-Hochelaga-Maisonneuve (Montreal), interview with author, October 2007.

12 *Montreal Gazette*, 30 January 2017, p. A4; *La Presse*, 30 May 2018.

13 *Montreal Gazette,* 28 March 2018, p. A4.
14 Bouchard, *Lettres,* pp. 102–3. Unless otherwise noted, all translations are the author's.
15 Ibid., pp. 89–90.
16 Duhaime, *L'État contre les jeunes,* p. 20.
17 Vinet and Filion, *Pauvreté et problèmes sociaux,* p. viii.

1 Identity

1 Spanish is spoken by 430 million, Arabic 420 million, Portuguese 220 million, and French 220 million.
2 Ravenna Aulakh, "Dying Languages: Scientists Fret as One Disappears Every 14 Days," *The Star,* 15 April 2013, https://www.thestar.com/news/world/2013/04/15/dying_languages_scientists_fret_as_one_disappears_every_14_days.html.
3 *Le Devoir,* 12 January 2016, p. A7.
4 Saint-Germain, *L'Avenir du bluff québécois,* pp. 85–6.
5 Bombardier, *Dictionnaire amoureux du Québec,* pp. 240–1.
6 Amartya Sen, *Identity and Violence: The Illusions of Destiny* (New York: Penguin, 2007), p. 19.
7 Ibid., pp. xiii–xiv.
8 Quoted in Scowen, *A Different Vision,* p. 153.
9 Payette, *Ce peuple,* pp. 37–40.
10 Laval du Breuil, "Nostalgie d'un Noël en français," *Le Devoir,* 22 January 2008.
11 Conversation with the author, March 1999.
12 Kipling, *Letters of Travel,* p. 123.
13 Claude Bélanger, "Quebec Act," Quebec History, 23 August 2000, http://faculty.marianopolis.edu/c.belanger/quebechistory/readings/1774act.htm.
14 Gossage and Little, *An Illustrated History of Quebec,* p. 72.
15 Ibid., pp. 79, 81, 83.
16 Courtois and Parenteau, *Les 50 discours,* p. 33.
17 Ibid., p. 35.
18 Frank McLynn, *1759: The Year Britain Became Master of the World* (London: Vintage, 2008), pp. 7–8.
19 Stephens, *Tony Blair,* p. 236.
20 Patten, *Not Quite the Diplomat: Home Truths about World Affairs* (London: Allan Lane, 2005), p. 27. The Entente Cordiale was the 1904 agreement that gave Britain a free hand in Egyptian affairs and France the same in Morocco.

21 Quoted in R.W. Johnson, "Danger: English Lessons," *London Review of Books*, 16 March 2017, pp. 24–6.

22 Reprinted in *New York Times*, 4 December 1893.

23 Johnson, "Danger: English Lessons," p. 231.

24 du Breuil, "Nostalgie d'un Noël en français."

25 Létourneau, *Le Québec entre son passé*, pp. 82–4.

26 Bombardier, *Dictionnaire amoureux du Québec*, p. 349.

27 Courtois and Parenteau, *Les 50 discours*, p. 49.

28 Dubuc, *À mes amis souverainistes*, p. 94.

29 Létourneau, *Le Québec entre son passé*, p. 131.

30 Ibid., pp. 141–3.

31 Ibid., pp. 9–12.

32 Ibid., pp. 16–17.

33 Maclure, *Quebec Identity*, p. 24.

34 Ibid., pp. 26–7.

35 Quoted in Maclure, *Quebec Identity*, pp. 32–5.

36 Ibid., pp. 37–45.

37 Ibid., p. 73.

38 Quoted in ibid., p. 74.

39 Payette and Payette, *Une fabrique de servitude*, pp. 81–5.

40 Quoted in Léger, Nantel, and Duhamel, *Le Code Québec*, p. 93.

41 Ignatieff, *Fire and Ashes*, p. 62.

42 Létourneau, *Le Québec entre son passé*, p. 70.

43 Speech of 18 July 1855, cited in Courtois and Parenteau, *Les 50 discours*, p. 88.

44 Marois, *Québécoise!*, p. 183.

45 Gaston Deschênes, "La devise 'Je me souviens,'" *Encyclopédia de l'Agora*, 1 April 2012, http://agora.qc.ca/documents/quebec_-_etat–la_devise_ je_me_souviens_par_gaston_deschenes/.

46 Létourneau, *Le Québec entre son passé*, pp. 87–110.

47 Michel Arseneault, email message to author, 20 December 2015.

48 Dubuc, *À mes amis souverainistes*, p. 69.

49 Study commissioned by the CSN, the Mouvement national des Québécois, the Société Saint-Jean-Baptiste, and the Mouvement Québec français, reported in *Le Devoir*, 27 January 2016, pp. A1, A10.

50 *Le Devoir*, 26 January 2016, pp. A1–A8.

51 Statistics Canada, "Census in Brief: English, French, and Official Language Minorities in Canada," 2 August 2017, http://www12.statcan.gc.ca/census-recensement/2016/as-sa/98-200-x/2016011/98-200-x2016011-eng.cfm.

52 *Gazette*, 17 January 2008, p. A10.

53 Elizabeth Redden, "Third Rail Issues," *Inside Higher Ed*, 24 March 2017, https://www.insidehighered.com/news/2017/03/24/head-mcgills-canadian-studies-institute-resigns-after-column-offensive-some/.

54 Quoted in Don Macpherson, "Andrew Potter and la famille québécoise," *Montreal Gazette*, 27 March 2017, http://montrealgazette.com/opinion/don-macpherson-andrew-potter-and-la-famille-quebecoise.

55 Ibid.

56 Pierre Fortin, interview with author, 15 March 2017.

57 Bombardier, *Dictionnaire amoureux du Québec*, p. 19.

58 Ibid., p. 76.

59 *Journal de Montréal*, 30 March 2016.

60 Lévesque, *My Quebec*, p. 8.

61 Quoted in Woodcock, *Confederation Betrayed*, p. 34.

62 Quoted in Maclure, *Quebec Identity*, p. 6.

63 Hébert, *The Morning After*, p. 32.

64 Bernard Landry, interview with author, 9 December 2015.

65 Rhéal Séguin, "Protocol 'Mistake' in Mexico Infuriates Bouchard," *The Globe and Mail*, 1 December 2000, https://www.theglobeandmail.com/news/national/protocol-mistake-in-mexico-infuriates-bouchard/article4169545/.

66 Payette and Payette, *Une fabrique de servitude*, p. 178.

67 *Le Devoir*, 21 November 2014, pp. A1, A12.

68 *Montreal Gazette*, 7 August 2017, p. A3.

69 *Montreal Gazette*, 19 January 2017, pp. A1–A3; *Le Devoir*, 19 January 2017, p. A2.

70 Philip Authier, "Quebecers Urged To Say Au Revoir to 'Bonjour-Hi'," *Montreal Gazette*, 16 November 2018, http://montrealgazette.com/news/quebec/parti-quebecois-motion-would-declare-bonjour-hi-an-irritant.

71 Behiels and Hayday, *Contemporary Quebec*, pp. 383–90.

72 *The Gazette*, 2 March 2008, p. A3.

73 Scowen, *Time to Say Goodbye*, p. 101. Also see Marian Scott, "Census 2016: English Is Making Gains in Quebec," *Montreal Gazette*, 2 August 2017, https://montrealgazette.com/news/local-news/census-2016-bilingualism-hits-all-time-high-in-quebec-zacross-canada.

74 Statistics Canada, "Census in Brief: Languages Used in the Workplace in Canada," 29 November 2017, https://www12.statcan.gc.ca/census-recensement/2016/as-sa/98-200-x/2016031/98-200-x2016031-eng.cfm.

75 Robert Vézina, president and CEO of OQLF, interview with author, 17 May 2017.

76 "Quebec women right-to-vote milestone marked by province," CBC News, 25 April 2015, https://www.cbc.ca/news/canada/montreal/quebec-women-right-to-vote-milestone-marked-by-province-1.3048852/.

77 Mills, *A Place in the Sun,* p. 38.
78 Laporte, *True Face of Duplessis,* p. 12.
79 Behiels and Hayday, *Contemporary Quebec,* pp. 182–94.
80 From Leclerc's autobiography *Moi, mes souliers,* quoted by Jean-François Nadeau in "Un pont Félix-Leclerc," *Le Devoir,* 21 December 2015.
81 Nadeau, "Un pont Félix-Leclerc," *Le Devoir,* 21 December 2015.
82 Behiels and Hayday, *Contemporary Quebec,* pp. 182–94.
83 Interview with author, 12 January 2016.
84 Charles Taylor, foreword to Maclure, *Quebec Identity,* pp. vii–viii.

2 Diversity

1 Mills, *A Place in the Sun,* p. 3.
2 Li Xu, "Who Drives a Taxi in Canada?" Citizenship and Immigration Canada, March 2012, http://www.cic.gc.ca/english/pdf/research-stats/taxi.pdf.
3 Lindsay Richardson, "Outcry Over a Perplexing Parade Video Blown Out of Proportion, Organizers Say," CTV News Montreal, 24 June 2017, http://montreal.ctvnews.ca/outcry-over-a-perplexing-parade-video-blown-out-of-proportion-organizers-say-1.3474839.
4 Dan Bilefsky, "A Show about Indigenous Canadians Has a Glaring Omisson: Indigenous Canadian Actors," *New York Times,* 16 June 2018, https://www.nytimes.com/2018/07/16/theater/robert-lepage-kanata-indigenous.html.
5 *Montreal Gazette,* 15 January 2016, p. A2. The survey was based on twenty-five-minute interviews with 1,501 people in April–June 2015.
6 *Montreal Gazette,* 10 November 2015, p. A4.
7 Vinet and Filion, *Pauvreté et problèmes sociaux,* pp. 20, 22.
8 Senator Pierre de Bané, conversation with author, 26 August 2007.
9 Pierre Fortin, interview with author, 15 March 2017.
10 White, *Here Is New York,* p. 47.
11 *Le Devoir,* 15 December 2015, pp. A1, A8.
12 *Montreal Gazette,* 25 September 2015, p. A13.
13 Quoted in La Rivière, *Enfin la laïcité,* p. 55.
14 The poster is on public display within the Musée d'art et d'histoire de Saint-Denis, Saint Denis (Seine-Saint-Denis) (viewed 22 April 2018).
15 "Austria Proposes Headscarf Ban for Girls under 10," BBC News, 4 April 2018, http://www.bbc.com/news/world-europe-43646560.
16 "Denmark Passes Ban on Niqabs and Burkas," BBC News, 31 May 2018, https://www.bbc.com/news/world-europe-44319921.

17 "The Islamic Veil across Europe," BBC News, 31 May 2018, http://www
.bbc.com/news/world-europe-13038095.

18 "Boris Johnson 'Won't Apologise' for Burka Comments," BBC News,
7 August 2018, https://www.bbc.co.uk/news/uk-politics-45096519.

19 Aurelien Breeden, "No Handshake, No Citizenship, French Court Tells
Algerian Woman," *New York Times*, 21 April 2018, https://www.nytimes
.com/2018/04/21/world/europe/handshake-citizenship-france.html.

20 *Le Devoir*, 15 January 2014.

21 La Rivière, *Enfin la laïcité*, p. 47.

22 Ibid., p. 105.

23 Calderisi, *Earthly Mission,*pp. 181–6.

24 *Montreal Gazette*, 9 February 2013, p. A6.

25 Quoted in La Rivière, *Enfin la laïcité*, pp. 129–31.

26 La Rivière, *Enfin la laïcité*, p. 63.

27 Quoted in La Rivière, *Enfin la laïcité*, p. 164.

28 La Rivière, *Enfin la laïcité*, p. 186.

29 Ibid., p. 31.

30 *Montreal Gazette*, 28 November 2007, p. A8.

31 *Montreal Gazette*, 29 November 2007, p. A8.

32 *Le Devoir*, 30 November 2007, p. A4.

33 Matthew Weaver, "Angela Merkel: German Multiculturalism Has 'Utterly
Failed,'" *The Guardian*, 17 October 2010, https://www.theguardian.com/
world/2010/oct/17/angela-merkel-german-multiculturalism-failed.

34 Rick Noack, "Multiculturalism Is a Sham, Says Angela Merkel," *Washington
Post*, 14 December 2015, https://www.washingtonpost.com/news/
worldviews/wp/2015/12/14/angela-merkel-multiculturalism-is-a-sham/.

35 The actual "scores" were: flag (86 per cent), armed forces (80 per cent),
hockey (71 per cent), multiculturalism (61 per cent), health system
(50 per cent) (Reitz, "Assessing Multiculturalism," p. 11).

36 Reitz, "Assessing Multiculturalism," p. 12.

37 Blanchet-Gravel, *Le Nouveau triangle amoureux*, p. 19.

38 Bernard Landry, interview with author, 9 December 2015.

39 Rattansi, *Multiculturalism*, pp. 39–40.

40 Reitz, "Assessing Multiculturalism," p. 167.

41 Ibid., p. 95.

42 Ibid., pp. 131–2.

43 Rattansi, *Multiculturalism*, pp. 73, 75–80, 93.

44 Sean Coughlan, "How Canada Became an Education Superpower," BBC
News, 2 August 2017, http://www.bbc.com/news/business-40708421.

45 Michel David, "Le Cheval de Troie," *Le Devoir*, 23 June 2017, http://www
.ledevoir.com/politique/quebec/501895/le-cheval-de-troie.

46 Ignatieff, *The Rights Revolution*, p. 37.

47 Quoted in Mathieu Bock-Côté, "René Lévesque sur l'immigration, l'identité et deux ou trois autres détails," *Journal de Montréal*, 9 October 2016.

48 Lisée, *Nous*, pp. 7–8.

49 *La Presse*, 27 May 2018.

50 Ibid., p. 8.

51 Ibid., pp. 11–12.

52 Bock-Côté, *Le Multiculturalisme*, p. 11.

53 Bombardier, *Dictionnaire amoureux du Québec*, p. 367.

54 Léger, Nantel, and Duhamel, *Le Code Québec*, pp. 79–80.

55 Terry Haig, email message to author, 30 November 2017.

56 Inam Malik, interview with author, 13 December 2017.

3 Solidarity

1 Ian Bennett, interview with author, 18 November 2016.

2 Michel David, *Le Devoir*, 26 April 2016, p. A3.

3 Duhaime, *L'État contre les jeunes*, pp. 38–9.

4 Payette, *Ce peuple*, p. 202n68.

5 Saint-Germain, *L'Avenir du bluff québécois*, p. 50.

6 Bombardier, *Dictionnaire amoureux du Québec*, p. 133.

7 Levine, *Health Care and Politics*, p. 16.

8 Hébert, *The Morning After*, p. 149.

9 Marois, *Québécoise!*, pp. 51–2.

10 Ibid., p. 77.

11 Léo Bureau-Blouin, interview with author, 10 March 2016.

12 *The Montreal Gazette*, 3 June 2016.

13 Bernard Landry, interview with author, 9 December 2015.

14 Michel David, "Les zélotes," *Le Devoir*, 22 January 2008, p. A3.

15 Saint-Germain, *L'Avenir du bluff québécois*, p. 82.

16 Ibid., pp. 85–6.

17 Jacques Dufresne, "Le Trublion de l'indépendance: Christian Saint-Germain," *Encyclopédie de L'Agora*, 22 September 2015, http://agora.qc.ca/documents/le_trublion_de_lindependance_christian_saint_germain.

18 Nadeau, *Bourgault*, pp. 354, 366.

19 David Yates, "Louis Laberge: Father of the Fonds," *Montreal Gazette*, 26 February 2013, http://www.montrealgazette.com/news/louis+laberge+father+fonds/8018941/story.html.

20 "Saint's remains moved to chapel she founded," *Globe and Mail,* 25 April 2005, https://www.theglobeandmail.com/news/national/saints-remains-moved-to-chapel-she-founded/article979257/.

21 Kevin Dougherty, "Impact on Quebecor Prompts Pierre Karl Péladeau to Appeal Conviction for Flouting Election Law," CBC News, 8 August 2014, https://www.cbc.ca/news/canada/montreal/peladeau-parti-quebecois-party-financing-elections-quebec-1.4776660.

22 Hazareesingh, *How the French Think,* pp. 7, 9.

23 Poliquin, *René Lévesque,* p. 11.

24 MacGregor, *Canadians,* p. 6.

25 Manon Massé, interview with author, 6 December 2016.

26 Payette, *Ce peuple,* pp. 102, 176.

27 Vinet and Filion, *Pauvreté et problèmes sociaux,* p. vii.

28 Ibid., p. 19.

29 Ibid., pp. 14–18.

30 Ibid., pp. 73, 82.

31 Ibid., p. 67.

32 Hughes, *Early Intervention,* pp. 126–8.

33 van den Berg et al., *Combating Poverty,* pp. 52–3.

34 Ibid., pp. 34–5.

35 Hughes, *Early Intervention,* p. 141–4.

36 Castonguay, *Santé,* pp. 20–33.

37 Levine, *Health Care and Politics,* p. 199.

38 Isabelle Porter, "Plus de 18 000 Québécois en attente de physiothérapie," *Le Devoir,* 30 October 2017, http://www.ledevoir.com/societe/sante/511623/temps-d-attente-en-physio.

39 Castonguay, *Santé,* pp. 20–33.

40 Ibid., p. 24.

41 Bacchus Barua, "Waiting Your Turn: Wait Times for Care in Canada, 2017 Report," Fraser Institute, 7 December 2017, https://www.fraserinstitute.org/studies/waiting-your-turn-wait-times-for-health-care-in-canada-2017?utm_source=Fraser-Institute-Enews&utm_campaign=Waiting-Your-Turn-2017&utm_medium=Fraser_Update&utm_content=Learn_More&utm_term=700.

42 Levine, *Health Care and Politics,* pp. 101, 135, 246–9.

43 Castonguay, *Santé,* p. 41.

44 Ibid., p. 20.

45 Duhaime, *L'État contre les jeunes,* pp. 79–80.

46 *Le Devoir,* 1 February 2016, p. A4.

47 Hughes, *Early Intervention,* pp. 105–6; *Le Devoir,* 19 January 2017, p. A3.

48 Hughes, *Early Intervention*, pp. 116–17.
49 *Le Devoir*, 1 February 2016, pp. A1–A8.
50 *Le Devoir*, 26 April 2016, p. A6.
51 Raphael Minder, "Guaranteed Income for All? Switzerland's Voters Say No Thanks," *New York Times*, 5 June 2016, https://www.nytimes.com/2016/06/06/world/europe/switzerland-swiss-vote-basic-income.html?_r=0.
52 Lévesque, *My Quebec*, pp. 43–4.
53 Roderick Benns, "Quebec, Canada: Government 'Hints at' Guaranteed Minimum Income in New Budget," Basic Income Earth Network, 31 March 2017, https://basicincome.org/news/2017/03/quebec-canada-governments-hints-at-guaranteed-minimum-income-in-new-budget.
54 *Le Devoir*, 17 November 2015, p. B1.

4 Efficiency

1 Duhaime, *Libérez-nous des syndicats*, pp. 15–18.
2 Marcotte, *Pour en finir*, p. 15.
3 Fortin, "La Révolution tranquille," pp. 87–133.
4 Coughlan, "How Canada Became an Education Superpower," BBC News, 2 August 2017, http://www.bbc.com/news/business-40708421.
5 Pierre Fortin, "Six observations," pp. 284–99.
6 Fortin, "La Révolution tranquille."
7 Pierre Fortin, interview with author, 15 March 2017.
8 "Quebec's Debt 'Worryingly High,' Report Says," CBC News, 11 March 2014, http://www.cbc.ca/news/business/quebec-s-debt-worryingly-high-report-says-1.2568355.
9 Samuel Stebbins, "Tax Policy: States with the Highest and Lowest Taxes," *USA Today*, 6 April 2018, https://www.usatoday.com/story/money/taxes/2018/04/06/states-highest-and-lowest-taxes-3-6/482944002/.
10 Sean Speer, Milagros Palacios, and Feixue Ren, "Quebec's Tax Competitiveness: A Barrier to Prosperity," Quebec Prosperity Initiative, September 2014, https://www.fraserinstitute.org/sites/default/files/quebecs-tax-competitiveness-a-barrier-to-prosperity.pdf.
11 Bélanger, *L'Économie du Québec*, p. 18.
12 Godbout et al., *Oser choisir maintenant*, p. 25.
13 Duhaime, *L'État contre les jeunes*, p. 34.
14 Auger, *25 Mythes à déboulonner*, p. 38.
15 Ibid., p. 138.

16 Duhaime, *L'État contre les jeunes,* pp. 85–7.
17 *Montreal Gazette,* 21 November 2014, p. A11.
18 Castonguay, *Santé,* pp. 102–4.
19 "Public Sector Employment, Wages and Salaries, Seasonally Unadjusted and Adjusted," Statistics Canada, http://www.statcan.gc.ca/tables-tableaux/sum-som/l01/cst01/govt62a-eng.htm.
20 The SAQ had 7,033 employees and total sales of $3.1 billion; the LCBO had 6,768 employees and total sales of $5.9 billion. See Duhaime, *La SAQ pousse le bouchon!,* p. 105, and updated information at http://www.lcbo.com/content/dam/lcbo/corporate-pages/about/pdf/LCBO_AR16-17-english.pdf and https://s7d9.scene7.com/is/content/SAQ/rapport-annuel-2017-fr.
21 Marie-Eve Fournier, "Québéc était prêt à se priver de revenus," *La Presse,* 2 August 2018, http://plus.lapresse.ca/screens/95cca687-f718-47c9-aef6-4562c8f6b536__7C___0.html?utm_medium=Email&utm_campaign=Internal+Share&utm_content=Screen.
22 Duhaime, *Libérez-nous des syndicats,* p. 124.
23 Bélanger, *L'Économie du Québec,* p. 8.
24 Jean-Luc Landry, "Pour améliorer le modèle québécois," in Lefebvre, *Maximiser le potentiel économique,* p. 177.
25 Beth Daley, "Climate Change Brings Blueberries – And Competition," *New York Times,* 2 October 2007, http://www.nytimes.com/2007/10/02/world/americas/02iht-berries.1.7713299.html?mcubz=3.
26 *Montreal Gazette,* 1 June 2016, p. NP3.
27 Shawn Donna, "Global Productivity Slowdown Risks Social Turmoil, IMF Warns," *Financial Times,* 3 April 2017, https://www.ft.com/content/3e5b4822-1882-11e7-a53d-df09f373be87.
28 Fortin, "Empêcher l'économie du Québec," in Lefebvre, *Maximiser le potential économique,* p. 16.
29 Bélanger, *L'Économie du Québec,* pp. 21, 101.
30 The global figures (1,595 in Quebec, 1,470 in France, and 1,370 in Germany) have been divided by fifty-two weeks and hence include holidays. See also Fortin, "Empêcher l'économie du Québec," in Lefebvre, *Maximiser le potential économique,* p. 23.
31 St-Maurice, "La productivité," in Lefebvre, *Maximiser le potentiel économique,* pp. 43–50.
32 Laflèche, "Une meilleure intégration des immigrants," in Lefebvre, *Maximiser le potential économique,* pp. 52–6.
33 *National Post,* 28 July 2017.
34 *Le Devoir,* 8 August 2017, pp. B1–B2.

35 *Le Devoir*, 3 November 2015, p. B4.
36 Radio-Canada Information, 8 September 2017. For more information, see the website: http://www.fondationalphabetisation.org.
37 Godbout, "Revoir la fiscalité," in Lefebvre, *Maximiser le potential économique,* pp. 105–19.
38 Jean-Michel Cousineau, "Redistribuer les revenus: Tout est dans la manière," in Lefebvre, *Maximiser le potential économique,* pp. 102–3.
39 Lefebvre, "Les grands centres urbains," in Lefebvre, *Maximiser le potential économique,* p. 160.
40 Léger, Nantel, and Duhamel, *Le Code Québec,* pp. 174–5.
41 Jean-Claude Cloutier, "Passer à l'acte: Le Québec en manque d'entrepreneurs," in Lefebvre, *Maximiser le potential économique,* pp. 135–45.
42 Pierre Fortin, "Empêcher l'économie du Québec de ralentir," in Lefebvre, *Maximiser le potential économique,* p. 23.
43 Nadeau-Dubois, *In Defiance,* p. 13.
44 Ibid., p. 46.
45 Ibid., pp. 130–1.
46 Bélanger, *L'Économie du Québec,* p. 213.
47 *Montreal Gazette,* 5 November 2015, p. B7.
48 "Bombardier Defers Executive Salary Rises amid Outcry," BBC News, 3 April 2017, http://www.bbc.com/news/world-us-canada-39484055.
49 *Montreal Gazette,* 27 November 2015, p. C6.
50 Pierre Fortin, interview with author, 15 March 2017.
51 *Le Devoir,* 13 September 2017, p. A7.
52 Castonguay, *Santé,* p. 42.
53 Bélanger, *L'Économie du Québec,* pp. 178–81.
54 Castonguay, *La Fin des vaches sacrées,* p. 39
55 Nadeau-Dubois, *In Defiance,* p. 62.
56 Payette, *Ce peuple,* pp. 188–9.
57 Marois, *Québécoise!,* p. 257.
58 Bélanger, *L'Économie du Québec,* pp. 183–4.
59 Fortin, "Dette du Québec."
60 Tommy Chouinard, "Une Part des surplus aux familles et aux aînés, annonce Legault," *La Presse,* 3 December 2018, https://www.lapresse.ca/actualites/politique/politique-quebecoise/201812/03/01-5206541-une-part-des-surplus-aux-familles-et-aux-aines-annonce-legault.php.
61 "Quebec Credit Rating Surpasses Ontario for First Time Ever," *Toronto Sun,* 17 June 2017, http://www.torontosun.com/2017/06/16/quebec-credit-rating-surpasses-ontario-for-first-time-ever.

62 Francis Vailles, "Exit la prime Québec pour emprunter." *La Presse,* 13 July 2018.

63 Jonathan Trudel, "Mieux vaut être jeune au Québec qu'en Ontario!" *L'Actualité,* 10 March 2016.

64 Langlois, *Le Québec change,* pp. 85–9, 99–101.

65 "List of Canadian Provinces and Territories by Gross Domestic Product," Wikipedia, https://en.wikipedia.org/wiki/List_of_Canadian_provinces_ and_territories_by_gross_domestic_product.

66 Dubuc, *À mes amis souverainistes,* pp. 158–9, 170, 177.

5 Climate

1 Guilbeault, *Alerte!,* pp. 119–21.

2 *Le Devoir,* 14 September 2017, p. A7.

3 Guilbeault, *Alerte!,* pp. 94–5.

4 *Financial Times,* 13 March 2015.

5 "UK Carbon Emissions Fall to Late-19th Century Levels," *Financial Times,* 6 March 2017, https://www.ft.com/content/2bc62cb8-004f-11e7-8d8e-a5e3738f9ae4. See also *Financial Times,* 3 January 2018.

6 Alister Doyle, "Sweden Sets Goal to Phase Out Greenhouse Gas Emissions by 2045," Reuters, 2 February 2017, https://www.reuters.com/article/climatechange-sweden/sweden-sets-goal-to-phase-out-greenhouse-gas-emissions-by-2045-idUSL5N1FN6F2.

7 Mousseau, *Gagner la guerre du climat,* pp. 73–5.

8 Kendra Pierre-Louis, "Greenhouse Gas Emissions Accelerate Like a 'Speeding Freight Train' in 2018," *New York Times,* 5 December 2018, https://www.nytimes.com/2018/12/05/climate/greenhouse-gas-emissions-2018.html?emc=edit_th_181206&nl=todaysheadlines&nlid=599928441206).

9 Daniel Cusick, "Fossil Fuel Subsidies Cost $5 Trillion Annually and Worsen Pollution," *Scientific American,* 19 May 2015, https://www.scientificamerican.com/article/fossil-fuel-subsidies-cost-5-trillion-annually-and-worsen-pollution/.

10 World Bank, *Inclusive Green Growth,* pp. 3–4.

11 Guilbeault, *Alerte!,* p. 92.

12 Bloomberg, *Climate of Hope,* p. 123.

13 Ibid., pp. 11–16, 87.

14 Unpublished paper delivered by Ottmar Edenhofer, Head of Research, Potsdam Institute for Climate Impact Research, at Symposium on Mission: Sustainability, PTH Sankt Georgen/Frankfurt, 26 March 2015.

15 Reid, *Climate Change and Human Development*, p. 5.
16 World Bank, *Inclusive Green Growth*, p. 2.
17 Bloomberg, *Climate of Hope*, p. 97.
18 Ibid., pp. 91, 94.
19 Helen Wong, "The East Is Turning Green," *Financial Times*, 1 August 2017, https://www.ft.com/content/3e6ac1dc-75e1-11e7-90c0-90a9d1bc9691.
20 Berry, *Our Only World*, pp. 71–2.
21 Catherine Montambeault, "Une Vent nouveau sur le changement climatique," *Actualité*, 8 October 2017, http://www.journaldemontreal .com/2017/10/08/un-vent-nouveau-sur-le-changement-climatique.
22 "Canada and the Kyoto Protocol," Wikipedia, https://en.wikipedia.org/ wiki/Canada_and_the_Kyoto_Protocol.
23 Mousseau, *Gagner la guerre du climat*, p. 37.
24 Françoise David, *La Presse*, 7 June 2018.
25 Mousseau, *Gagner la guerre du climat*, pp. 247–8.
26 Guilbeault, *Alerte!*, pp. 129–30, 133.
27 *Le Devoir*, 14 September 2017, pp. B1–B2.
28 Auger, *25 Mythes à déboulonner*, p. 124.
29 *Montreal Gazette*, 28 November 2015, p. A3.
30 *Montreal Gazette*, 6 February 2016, p. A8.
31 Jacques Gérin, email message to author, 30 November 2017.
32 "Canada and the Kyoto Protocol," Wikipedia, https://en.wikipedia.org/ wiki/Canada_and_the_Kyoto_Protocol.
33 *Montreal Gazette*, 10 December 2015, p. A2.
34 Guilbeault, *Alerte!*, p. 211; Bloomberg, *Climate of Hope*, p. 21.
35 Bloomberg, *Climate of Hope*, pp. 20–1.
36 Dave Lank, "Quebec, the Climate Change Fighter," *Corporate Knights*, 11 October 2017, http://www.corporateknights.com/channels/ leadership/quebec-climate-change-fighter-15076980/.
37 Mousseau, *Gagner la guerre du climat*, pp. 247–8.
38 Guilbeault, *Alerte!*, pp. 200–5.
39 Mousseau, *Gagner la guerre du climat*, pp. 25–6.
40 Ibid., pp. 76–80.
41 Ibid., pp. 85–6.
42 Ibid., p. 13.
43 Guilbeault, *Alerte!*, p. 221.
44 Tracy McNicoll, "'End of the World' vs. 'End of the Month': Macron Walks Tightrope amid Fuel Tax Protests," *France 24*, 27 November 2018, https://www.france24.com/en/20181127-france-climate-yellow-vests-macron-fuel-tax-protests-nuclear-melenchon-pen-faure.

45 Denis Lessard, "Après les belles paroles, les gestes surivront-ils?" *La Presse*, 21 November 2018, http://mi.lapresse.ca/screens/075d4c18-1574-45a9-9e6b-d9ce6d1ebb27__7C___0.html.

6 Fairness

1 *Montreal Gazette*, 17 November 2006.
2 van Parijs and Vanderborght, *Basic Income*, p. 51.
3 Ibid., p. 77.
4 Ibid., pp. 86–7.
5 Ibid., p. 89.
6 Benns, *Basic Income*, p. ii.
7 Ibid., p. 57.
8 van Parijs and Vanderborght, *Basic Income*, p. 3.
9 Ibid., p. 45.
10 Benns, *Basic Income*, pp. 10, 239.
11 Ontario Basic Income Pilot, 7 September 2018, https://www.ontario.ca/page/ontario-basic-income-pilot.
12 "Canada's Ontario Government Cuts Basic Income Project Short," BBC News, 1 August 2018, https://www.bbc.co.uk/news/world-us-canada-45023510.
13 van Parijs and Vanderborght, *Basic Income*, pp. 167–8.
14 Benns, *Basic Income*, p. 155.
15 Ibid., pp. 21, 23, 26, 28.
16 Ibid., p. 64.
17 Ibid., p. 118.
18 Jessica Chin, "Most Canadians Think People Are Poor Due to Circumstance: Angus Reid Institute Survey," *Huffington Post*, 2 August 2018, https://www.huffingtonpost.ca/2018/08/02/canadians-poverty-angus-reid-institute_a_23494574/.
19 Caroline Plante, "Quebec Expert Panel Proposes Welfare Boost, but Stops Short of Minimum Income," *Montreal Gazette*, 13 November 2017, http://montrealgazette.com/news/local-news/improve-welfare-raise-work-premium-for-low-income-earners-quebec-panel.
20 "Factbox: Italy Votes for 62nd Government since World War Two," Reuters, 13 April 2008, https://www.reuters.com/article/us-italy-election-rules/factbox-italy-votes-for-62nd-government-since-world-war-two-idUSL135128120080413.
21 Potter, Weinstock, and Loewen, *Should We Change How We Vote?*, p. 97.

22 Ibid., p. 7.
23 Ibid., pp. 84–5.
24 Aaron Wherry, "Opposition Accuses Trudeau of 'Betrayal' as Liberals Abandon Promise of Electoral Reform," CBC News, 1 February 2017, http://www.cbc.ca/news/politics/trudeau-electoral-reform-mandate-1.3961736.
25 "Un Scrutin proportionnel au Québec: Jamais de votre vie?" Radio-Canada, 18 February 2017, http://ici.radio-canada.ca/nouvelle/1017622/mode-scrutin-proportionnel-reforme-difficile.
26 Marcel Blanchet and Jean-Pierre Kingsley, "Mode de scrutin il est temps de faire preuve d'audace," La Presse, 10 November 2018, http://mi.lapresse.ca/screens/4ea2d4b2-63a4-457f-8b3a-7f7cfb8f70b7__7C___0.html.

7 Looking Ahead

1 Lévesque, My Quebec, p. 132.
2 Duhaime, La SAQ pousse le bouchon!, p. 54.
3 James quoted in Virginia Woolf, The Death of the Moth (New York: Harcourt, Brace, 1942), pp. 132–3.
4 Bernanos, Nous autres Français, pp. 9–10.
5 Langlois, Le Québec change, p. 282.
6 Jacob Serebrin, "Quebec Losing 7,000 Residents to Other Provinces Every Year: Analysis," Montreal Gazette, 8 December 2017, https://montrealgazette.com/news/local-news/quebec-losing-7000-residents-to-other-provinces-every-year-analysis.
7 Lévesque quoted by Mathieu Bock-Côté, "René Lévesque sur l'immigration, l'identité et deux ou trois autres détails," Journal de Montréal, 9 October 2016.
8 Charles Taylor, foreword to Maclure, Quebec Identity, p. viii.
9 Létourneau, Le Québec entre son passé, pp. 51, 53–4.
10 Létourneau, "Remembering (From) Where You Are Going," p. 736.
11 Jacques, La Fatigue politique, p. 136.
12 Ibid., p. 57
13 Ibid., pp. 94–6.
14 Gérard Bouchard, "Repos nécessaire pour Jacques Beauchemin et ses mauvaises ides," Le Devoir, 13 July 2015, http://www.ledevoir.com/non-classe/444922/repos-necessaire-pour-jacques-beauchemin-et-ses-mauvaises-idees.
15 Dubuc, À mes amis souverainistes, pp. 206, 229–30.

16 According to the last census (2016), 94.5 per cent of Quebeckers are able to conduct a conversation in English and 87.1 per cent speak French at home, up slightly from the previous census.

17 Bombardier, *Dictionnaire amoureux du Québec*, p. 16.

18 Denise Bombardier, "Why Not?," *Le Devoir*, 19 January 2008.

19 Lisée, *Nous*, pp. 51–6.

20 Langlois, *Le Québec change*, p. 277.

21 Lisée, *Nous*, pp. 40, 42, 93.

22 Survey of May 2013, summarized in Langlois, *Le Québec change*, pp. 143–5.

23 Guy Sprung, "The Invisible 'Anglos' on the Quebec Theatre Scene," *Montreal Gazette*, 14 September 2017, http://montrealgazette.com/entertainment/theatre/guy-sprung-the-invisible-anglos-on-the-quebec-theatre-scene.

24 Kamila Hinkson, "Alexandre Cloutier Defends Holiday Greeting to Muslim Quebecers," CBC News, 14 July 2016, http://www.cbc.ca/news/canada/montreal/alexandre-cloutier-jean-francois-lisee-eid-message-1.3679427.

25 Hassan Guillet, "Attentat à la Grande Mosquée de Québec: Où en sommes-nous un an plus tard?" *La Presse*, 13 January 2018.

26 Denis Lessard, "Émotif dans ses adieux, Couillard fait un plaidoyer pour l'inclusion," *La Presse*, 4 October 2018, https://www.lapresse.ca/actualites/politique/politique-quebecoise/201810/04/01-5199056-emotif-dans-ses-adieux-couillard-fait-unplaidoyer-pour-linclusion.php.

27 Jacob Serebrin, "Montreal's Economy Is Hot. Now How Do We Get It Even Hotter?" *Montreal Gazette*, 30 July 2018, https://montrealgazette.com/news/local-news/montreals-economy-is-hot-now-how-do-we-get-it-even-hotter.

28 Langlois, *Le Québec change*, pp. 245–9.

29 Léger, Nantel, and Duhamel, *Le Code Québec*, pp. 201–2.

30 Marois, *Québécoise!*, p. 257.

31 Report of HEC, Montreal, reported in *Le Devoir*, 26 January 2016, pp. B1–B4.

32 Pierre Goulet, email message to author, 25 October 2017.

33 Castonguay, *La Fin des vaches sacrées*, pp. 55–6.

34 Sara Champagne, "Une Réduction du temps d'attente, mais à quel prix?" *La Presse*, 19 July 2018, http://plus.lapresse.ca/screens/b069be52-b08f-45ce-9e4c-29d559e67288__7C___0.html?utm_medium=Email&utm_campaign=Internal+Share&utm_content=Screen.

35 Castonguay, *La Fin des vaches sacrées*, p. 201.

36 Duhaime, *L'État contre les jeunes*, p. 74.

37 Marissa Groguhé, "Les Inquiétudes des qubécois plus près de la réalité, affirme une étude," *La Presse,* 19 June 2018, http://plus.lapresse.ca/ screens/10d229da-7b63-42a9-b1e0-620f9a007593__7C___0.html?utm_ medium=Email&utm_campaign=Internal+Share&utm_content=Screen.
38 "Creating a Better Health System: Lessons from Norway and Sweden," *The Conversation,* 1 September 2014, http://theconversation.com/ creating-a-better-health-system-lessons-from-norway-and-sweden-30366.
39 Survey of May 2013, described in Langlois, *Le Québec change,* p. 165.
40 Langlois, *Le Québec change,* pp. 154, 174.
41 Dale Eisler, *False Expectations: Politics and the Pursuit of the Saskatchewan Myth* (Regina: University of Regina Press, 2006), p. ix.
42 Castonguay, *La Fin des vaches sacrées,* pp. 184–5.

Bibliography

Auger, Michel G. *25 Mythes à déboulonner*. Montreal: Les Éditions de La Presse, 2018.

Bélanger, Gérard. *L'Économie du Québec, Mythes et Réalité*. Montreal: Varia, 2007.

Behiels, Michael D., and Matthew Hayday. *Contemporary Quebec: Selected Readings and Commentaries*. Montreal/Kingston McGill-Queen's University Press, 2011.

Benns, Roderick. *Basic Income: How a Canadian Movement Could Change the World*. Cambridge, ON: Fireside, 2016.

Bernanos, Georges. *Nous autres Français*. Paris: Gallimard, 1939.

Berry, Wendell. *Our Only World: Ten Essays*. Berkeley: Counterpoint, 2015.

Blanchet-Gravel, Jérôme. *Le Nouveau triangle amoureux: Gauche, islam et multiculturalisme*. Montreal: Accent Grave, 2013.

Bloomberg, Michael. *Climate of Hope: How Cities, Businesses, and Citizens Can Save the Planet*. New York: St. Martin's Press, 2017.

Bock-Côté, Mathieu, *Le Multiculturalisme comme religion politique*. Paris: Les Éditions du Cerf, 2016.

– "René Lévesque sur l'immigration, l'identité et deux ou trois autres détails." *Journal de Montréal*, 9 October 2016.

Bock-Côté, Mathieu, Charles-Philippe Courtois, Guillaume Marois, Guillaume Rousseau, and Patrick Sabourin. *Indépendance: Les conditions du Renouveau*. Montreal: VLB Éditeur, 2014.

Bombardier, Denise. *Dictionnaire amoureux du Québec*. Paris: Plon, 2014.

Bouchard, Lucien. *Lettres à un jeune politicien*. Montreal: VLB Éditeur, 2012.

Calderisi, Robert. *Earthly Mission: The Catholic Church and World Development*. New Haven: Yale University Press, 2013.

Castonguay, Claude. *La Fin des vaches sacrées: Réflexions sur l'avenir du Québec*. Montreal: Les Éditions La Presse, 2015.

– *Santé: L'heure des choix*. Montreal: Boréal, 2012.

Cather, Willa. *Shadows on the Rock*. 1931.

Courtois, Charles-Philippe, and Danic Parenteau. *Les 50 discours qui ont marqué le Québec*. Anjou: Les Éditions CEC, 2011.

Dubuc, Alain. *À mes amis souverainistes*. Montreal: Les Éditions Voix Parallèles, 2008.

Duhaime, Éric. *L'État contre les jeunes: Comment les baby-boomers ont détourné le système*. Montreal: VLB Éditeur, 2011.

– *Libérez-nous des syndicats*. Quebec: Les Éditions Genex, 2013.

– *La SAQ pousse le bouchon!* Montreal: VLB Éditeur, 2014.

Fortin, Pierre. "Dette du Québec: Plaidoyer pour la prudence." *L'Actualité*, 6 October 2014.

– "Empêcher l'économie du Québec de ralentir." In Lefebvre, *Maximiser le potential économique*, pp. 15–25.

– "La Révolution tranquille et l'économie: Ou étions-nous, que visions-nous, qu'avons-nous accompli?" In *La Révolution tranquille en héritage*, edited by Guy Berthiaume and Claude Corbo. Montreal: Boréal, 2011.

– "Six observations sur la croissance québécoise à la manière de Gilles Paquet." In *Gilles Paquet, homo hereticus*, edited by Ruth Hubbard and Jeffrey Roy, pp. 284–99. Ottawa: Presses de l'Université d'Ottawa, 2009.

Fraser, Graham. *Sorry, I Don't Speak French: Confronting the Canadian Crisis That Won't Go Away*. Toronto: Douglas Gibson, 2007.

Godbout, Luc. "Revoir la fiscalité." In Lefebvre, *Maximiser le potential économique*, pp. 105–19.

Godbout, Luc, Pierre Fortin, Matthieu Arseneau, and Suzie St-Cerny. *Oser choisir maintenant: Des pistes de solution pour proteéger les services publics et assurer l'équité entre les generations*. Quebec: Les Presses de l'Université de Laval, 2007.

Gossage, Peter, and Jack Little. *An Illustrated History of Quebec: Tradition and Modernity*. Toronto: Oxford University Press, 2012.

Guilbeault, Steven. *Alerte! Le Québec à l'heure des changements climatiques*. Montreal: Boréal, 2009.

Hazareesingh, Sudhir. *How the French Think: An Affectionate Portrait of an Intellectual People*. London: Allen Lane, 2015.

Hébert, Chantal. *The Morning After: The 1995 Quebec Referendum and the Day That Almost Was*. Toronto: Alfred A. Knopf, 2014.

Hémon, Louis. *Maria Chapdelaine*. Paris: Nelson, 1934.

Howard, R.T. *Power and Glory: France's Secret Wars with Britain and America, 1945–2016*. London: Biteback, 2016.

Hughes, James. *Early Intervention: How Canada's Social Programs Can Work Better, Save Lives, and Often Save Money*. Toronto: James Lorimer, 2015.

Hutchison, Bruce. *The Unknown Country: Canada and Her People*. Toronto: Oxford University Press, 1942.

Ignatieff, Michael. *Fire and Ashes: Success and Failure in Politics*. Toronto: Random House, 2013.

– *The Rights Revolution*. Toronto: House of Anansi, 2004.

Jacques, Daniel. *La Fatigue politique du Québec français*. Montreal: Boréal, 2008.

Kipling, Rudyard. *Letters of Travel (1892–1913)*. London: Macmillan, 1927.

Laflèche, Thérèse. "Une meilleure intégration des immigrants au marché du travail." In Lefebvre, *Maximiser le potentiel économique*, pp. 51–65.

Langlois, Simon. *Le Québec change: Chroniques sociologiques*. Del Busso: Montreal, 2017.

Laporte, Pierre. *The True Face of Duplessis*. Montreal: Harvest House, 1960.

La Rivière, Bernard. *Enfin la laïcité*. Montreal: Les Éditions XYZ, 2014.

Lefebvre, Mario. "Les grands centres urbains comme moteur économique du Québec." In Lefebvre, *Maximiser le potentiel économique*, pp. 159–71.

Lefebvre, Mario, ed. *Maximiser le potentiel économique du Québec: Treize réflexions*. Quebec: Les Presses de l'Université Laval, 2016.

Léger, Jean-Marc, Jacques Nantel, and Pierre Duhamel. *Le Code Québec: Les sept differences qui font de nous un peuple unique au monde*. Montreal: Les Éditions de l'Homme, 2016.

Létourneau, Jocelyn. *Le Québec entre son passé et ses passages*. Montreal: Fides, 2010.

– "Remembering (From) Where You Are Going: Memory as Legacy and Inheritance." In *Contemporary Quebec: Selected Readings and Commentaries*, edited by Michael D. Behiels and Matthew Hayday, pp. 730–54. Montreal/Kingston: McGill-Queen's University Press, 2011.

Lévesque, René. *My Quebec*. Toronto: Methuen, 1979.

Levine, David. *Health Care and Politics*. Montreal: Véhicule, 2015.

Linteau, Paul-André. *Histoire du Québec contemporain*. Vol. 1, *De la Confédération à la crise (1867–1929)*. Montreal: Boréal, 1989.

Lisée, Jean-François. *Nous*. Montreal: Boréal, 2007.

MacGregor, Roy. *Canadians: A Portrait of a Country and Its People*. Toronto: Viking, 2007.

Maclure, Jocelyn. *Quebec Identity: The Challenge of Pluralism*. Translated by Peter Feldstein. Montreal/Kingston: McGill-Queen's University Press, 2003. Originally published as *Récits identitaires: Le Québec à l'épreuve du pluralism*. Montreal: Québec Amérique, 2000.

Marcotte, Joanne. *Pour en finir avec le Gouvernemaman.* Montreal: Éditions Francine Breton, 2011.

Marois, Pauline. *Québécoise!* Montreal: Fides, 2008.

McLynn, Frank. *1759: The Year Britain Became Master of the World.* London: Vintage, 2008.

Mills, Sean. *A Place in the Sun: Haiti, Haitians, and the Remaking of Quebec.* Montreal/Kingston: McGill-Queen's University Press: 2016.

Mousseau, Normand. *Gagner la guerre du climat: Douze mythes à déboulonner.* Montreal: Boréal, 2017.

Nadeau, Jean-François. *Bourgault.* Montreal: Lux Éditeur, 2007.

Nadeau-Dubois, Gabriel. *In Defiance.* Toronto: Between the Lines, 2015.

Patten, Chris. *Not Quite the Diplomat: Home Truths about World Affairs.* London: Allan Lane, 2005.

Payette, Jean-François. *Ce peuple qui ne fut jamais souverain: La tentation du suicide politique des Québécois.* Montreal: Les Éditions Fides, 2013.

Payette, Roger, and Jean-François Payette. *Une fabrique de servitude: La condition culturelle des Québécois.* EFIDES, 2015.

Poliquin, Daniel. *René Lévesque.* Montreal: Boréal, 2009.

Potter, Andrew, Daniel Weinstock, and Peter Loewen. *Should We Change How We Vote? Evaluating Canada's Electoral System.* Montreal/Kingston: McGill-Queen's University, 2017.

Rattansi, Ali. *Multiculturalism: A Very Short Introduction.* Oxford: Oxford University Press, 2011.

Reid, Hannah. *Climate Change and Human Development.* London: Zed, 2014.

Reitz, Jeffrey G. "Assessing Multiculturalism as a Behavioural Theory." In *Multiculturalism and Social Cohesion: Potentials and Challenges of Diversity,* edited by Jeffrey G. Reitz, Raymond Breton, Karen Kisiel Dion, and Kenneth L. Dion. Springer, 2009.

Saint-Germain, Christian. *L'Avenir du bluff québécois: La chute d'un people hors de l'Histoire.* Montreal: Liber, 2015.

Scowen, Reed. *A Different Vision: The English in Quebec in the 1990s.* Toronto: McClelland and Stewart, 1991.

– *Time to Say Goodbye.* Toronto: McClelland and Stewart, 2007.

Sen, Amartya. *Identity and Violence: The Illusions of Destiny.* New York: Penguin, 2007.

Statistics Canada. "Public Sector Employment, Wages and Salaries, Seasonally Unadjusted and Adjusted." Table 10-10-0025-01. http://www.statcan.gc.ca/tables-tableaux/sum-som/l01/cst01/govt62a-eng.htm.

Stephens, Philip. *Tony Blair: The Making of a World Leader.* London: Viking, 2004.

St-Maurice, Yves. "La productivité." In Lefebvre, *Maximiser le potential économique*, pp. 41–9.

van den Berg, Axel, Charles Plante, Hicham Raïq, Christine Proulx, and Sam Faustmann. *Combating Poverty: Quebec's Pursuit of a Distinctive Welfare State.* Toronto: University of Toronto Press, 2017.

van Parijs, Philippe, and Yannick Vanderborght. *Basic Income: A Radical Proposal for a Free Society and a Sane Economy.* Cambridge, MA: Harvard University Press, 2017.

Vinet, Jocelyn, and Danielle Filion. *Pauvreté et problèmes sociaux.* Montreal: Fides Éducation, 2015.

White, E.B. *Here Is New York.* New York: Little Bookroom, 1949.

Woodcock, George. *Confederation Betrayed: The Case against Trudeau's Canada.* Madeira Park: Harbour, 1981.

Woolf, Virginia. *The Death of the Moth.* New York: Harcourt, Brace, 1942.

World Bank. *Inclusive Green Growth: The Pathway to Sustainable Development.* Washington, DC: World Bank, 2012.

Index